# THE
# ARCHER

## CAROL COTTONE CHOOMACK

authorHOUSE®

*AuthorHouse™ LLC*
*1663 Liberty Drive*
*Bloomington, IN 47403*
*www.authorhouse.com*
*Phone: 1-800-839-8640*

*Author photo credit : EMMA PITTS*

*Published by AuthorHouse 10/31/2013*

*ISBN: 978-1-4918-1586-1 (sc)*
*ISBN: 978-1-4918-1587-8 (hc)*
*ISBN: 978-1-4918-1588-5 (e)*

*Library of Congress Control Number: 2013916292*

# *Dedication*

*I* thank all of my dearest friends who rode this wave with me for the past fifteen months. You generously gave me your time, expertise, and support, happily encouraging me on my journey. You stoked the fire in me, pushing me with wonderful words of reassurance, never letting me doubt myself. Tonya, you kept my flame alive through it all; you were my strength when I faltered, my confidante and forever my friend. I thank you. Twiggy what would I have done without you? Your expertise in formatting, sizing photos and knowledge of proper submission guidelines saved me from un-nerving panic. To my sister Beth for her ever encouraging words and to my lifelong friend, Suzie thank you for listening when I needed an ear.

Tonya Heartsong
Twiggy Girouard
Beth Cottone
Suzie Ventres

*I* was directed to this place by the hand and voice of God. Herein, I have used my gift in giving and love, having reached into my soul, centering my creativity and intuition to bring this book to life. This writing of *The Archer* has been my perfect journey, for in it, I have met a very special man, a teacher and guide whose extraordinary life and way opened my world and my heart to new wisdom and awareness.

# Table of Contents

# Acknowledgments

All things have a time of happening.
There is nothing left to chance.

*A* very special thank you to Armin Michael Hirmer for trusting me and for all the knowledge he has so generously shared, for without him, there would be no tale to tell. He has been my inspiration and guide on this amazing journey. I have found him to possess facets like those of a diamond and the wisdom of one who has lived a thousand years. Yes, he is a man of modern times; his soul is pure, and his intent is to guide with gentle strength. A disciplined man, he lives simply. He is committed to living in harmony and balance with all of life. Armin brings peacefulness in knowing of love, hope, and compassion to those who have entered his world by uniting souls with the use of his bow and arrows. He is of empty-mindedness, connected to his inner being, and in that, he is profoundly connected to God. Armin has chosen to live his life now as teacher and guide, rooted to the earth, he watches the oceans and the heavens realizing his place in the universe, accepting what is. You will come to understand his sensitive heart and know the message he sends to all who are graced by knowing him.

*"To see is to believe. To know is of the heart."*

It is with a humble enthusiasm that I have written this story of a man living among us. With the click of a mouse, I came to find him within the confines of my modern silver machine. It was not by chance, as I knew better than that. Nothing in life occurs by chance. It was a universal vibration radiating and my ability to capture what was revealed to my eyes. His photography spoke a million words. His eyes of azure blue mesmerized me; within them, I saw a million oceans rippling the spirit within him.

He trusted me enough to bare his soul in the telling of a small part of his life's tale. I wondered who this person could be to share himself and his soul with one he does not know. I shall never betray his trust and will tell you of him in the most honorable way.

This story will take you on a journey of his travels, revealing the light that lies within him. He has but one suitcase and no home to call his own. He carries his bow and arrows wherever he goes, and in this, he is rich beyond all measure.

He is *the Archer* and so much more.

I am grateful for the gift of life and pleased to present to you this mystical tale.

A story will unravel before you,
one of fact and fiction.

# Preface

*B*avaria is located in the south of Germany. It is known as an exceptional part of the country. Its beauty and its historic value are recognized worldwide. During the period from 1135 to 1136, a stone bridge was built across the Danube River at Regensburg, opening international trade routes between Northern Europe and Venice. Many wealthy trading families settled there, beginning Regensburg's Golden Age. Bavaria is the homeland of great cathedrals and castles. Its architecture is a mixture of twentieth-century modern and that of times long past the gothic style, which is both elegant and regal. You will find winding roads romance the path they follow through cities and villages, while looming mountains touch the sky and reach into floating clouds as the images of the Bavarian Alps are mirrored in the ten-thousand-year-old glacial lakes below. Germany itself is the home of Albert Einstein and the Brothers Grimm, creators of the fairy tales *Hansel and Gretel*, *Rumplestiltskin*, and *Snow White*, to name a few. The inspiration and filming for *The Sound of Music*, a 1965 American film directed by Robert Wise, took place in Austria and Bavaria.

Photo by Armin Hirmer

# I Choose

I choose to live by choice,
not by chance.

I choose to make changes,
not excuses.

I choose to be motivated,
not manipulated.

I choose to be useful,
not used.

I choose to excel,
not compete.

I choose self-esteem,
not self-pity.

I choose to listen
To my inner voice,
not the random opinion of others.

By Jacqueline Witt
Shortened from the original and used with permission

.

## Chapter One

# The Archer

*T*he ancient German village of Burglengenfeld has a population of approximately twelve thousand and is located in the district of Schwandorf, Bavaria. A grand castle built in the eighteenth century by a family of nobility maintains a daunting presence there, with an eeriness of medieval times, of knights and legends, lingering behind. Burglengenfeld Castle, a historic remnant of the past, is perched high atop a hillside overlooking rows of closely knit, aged houses made of stone and brick. It keeps a careful watch on the tranquil town below, which is nestled close to the winding River Naab near the Bavarian Forest. This village has a feeling of antiquity with its fine, intricately designed buildings. Carved moldings grace the grandeur of local ancient cathedrals, showing off an impressive artistry not often used in modern times.

A child was born there in the mid-1960s, one who would make a difference in the lives of many. His eyes were a captivating blue; his hair, although sparse at birth, promised to be blond. His given name was Armin, meaning to be whole, immense, and universal. Time would prove this name suited the child and man he would become. His birth brought great joy to his parents, who were hardworking, upstanding middle-class citizens. He had a happy and normal upbringing by all accounts. Indeed, the economics of the time during his early childhood did not permit extras and certainly none of the frills some of his friends enjoyed. He paid no mind to such things and was left to use his imagination and creativity to fill the void of his wanting. Both his parents worked away from home, leaving little time for substance in nurturing. Armin was strong-willed in a gentle way and very self-sufficient, having to do most things on his own. He learned at an early age how to fend for himself. There were intervals when he tried to ignore the emotions of loneliness he felt, wishing to spend more time with his parents, who were lost in their busy schedules. Armin understood and appreciated their hard work and need to provide for the family. He received enough attention and love to instill principles and a code of ethics that would last a lifetime. As a young boy, he gained knowledge of many things. He watched and listened in silence, learning all he could from those around him.

Striving to provide a better way of life for their family, Armin's father accepted a position in Regensburg working in a new manufacturing company. It was there that Armin began school. He loved learning, and as he grew, reading became his favorite pastime. Armin knew worldly things beyond his age, things that were not taught in academic courses. Considered to be a hardworking and popular leader in his class, Armin never considered himself any different from others. He had a love of art and drawing, which brought him to a place of knowing that one day, these gifts would be an intricate part of his daily life. Germany's splendid architecture greatly influenced him. There were many years of education ahead of him, and he showed early success and great promise for his future. Armin found balance and harmony in all things in life, knowing at an early age that the ease of flow was vital to the person he was. His parents taught him respect, which he gave to his teachers, peers, and others in his life. He soon found that what he gave was exactly what he received. Unknowingly, he was already engaged in the lessons of life, leaving him a sense of pride in the way he chose to live.

Armin was an intellectual, and his mind focused on many subject matters. From his youngest days, he discovered that his thoughts created his reality. He learned that a positive attitude and a heartfelt desire could simply turn the world in his favor. There were days when he didn't want to go to classes and would argue the point with his mother, giving all kinds of reasons as to why he should stay home. Armin could easily create a headache, stomachache, or nausea with a simple thought, leaving his eyes droopy and his skin pale, like white bread. This was an awakening for him. "If I can make myself sick, then I can make myself well. It is my mind that controls everything," he said. Focused, he knew the course he would take.

In time, Armin studied martial arts and the mind, experimenting with strident disciplines. By doing this, he would attain all he desired. Respectfully, he listened to those older and wiser than he, thinking that their experiences and advice were absolute and would lead him to the right path. It took him time to understand that his voice mattered greatly and the revelations he had stumbled upon had tremendous merit. While listening to others, Armin realized he had the right to make his own choices along life's journey. And he did.

Intervals in his growth passed too quickly, and the years of youthful innocence were inevitably gone too soon. Aware of the fragility of time, Armin lived only in the moment that presented itself. From his early childhood, he spent more time in nature watching birds and animals than he did with others. He found a special connection with nature that he could not find with his friends. Often, he would go off into the woods near his home where a hidden lake teemed with birds and forest animals. It was a place that brought new life into him. There, he was free, able to lose himself in the luxury of solitude. He pushed all thoughts from his head, becoming empty-minded, and found an inexplicable sense of peace and quiet away from the rest of the world. In the silence, he watched miracles made from another's hand, the hand of God, unfold. His books and school lessons were with him, but his mind was always distracted by the subtle sounds that filled the atmosphere and the wind that blew gently, rearranging his long blond hair. Taking a deep breath, he relished the smell of wildflowers and the scent of ancient pine trees. Reaching down beside him, he placed his hands deep into the soft forest floor and brought a handful of sod near his face to smell the richness of Mother Earth. Her nurturing effects were profound, and gratitude stirred within him. Sitting in this magical place, he viewed his private pond, escaping from the world's reality and all the noises that had never made particular sense to him. Armin found great joy connecting to the mysticism of the universe.

Suddenly, a splash in the water sent ripples across the pond, startling him. Nearby, songbirds filled Armin's head with their music, and he nodded as if to conduct the symphony of sounds that filled his private world. Amused, he watched a newly arrived flock of Canada geese dip their heads below the water's surface. They bobbed in and out of oblivion carefree and trusting of him. Awaking from his peaceful trance, he found several geese ambling toward him, squawking as they waddled near. To his left, several had already gathered and were sitting next to him without any hint of fear. Cautiously reaching into his pocket, he pulled from it pieces of bread, a gift offering he had brought with him. Happily, they took the food from his hand as he spoke to them much like an old friend. They sat listening to the different intonations and rich timbre of Armin's resonating voice. Each cocked their heads from one side to the other as if to understand his every word. Appreciating the beauty of nature, Armin was comfortable during these times in the forest, knowing the path ahead would be guided by the flow of the universe.

Lost in thought, he fell back on his elbows, listening to the soft sounds floating easily with the stirring of the wind and the gentle squabble of his winged friends. Voices nearby startled him. There was a disturbance ahead, and the muffled barking of hounds stirred the air. Squinting his eyes, Armin tried to find a clear view through the misty light that filtered from above, streaming through the tall, gnarled prehistoric-looking trees. The denseness of the woodland lent a feeling of creepiness, as tangled moss in hues of pale white and green swayed in the breeze, reaching and stretching downward to touch the earth. His vision was fuzzy, as if he were looking through the dirty lens of a camera, unclear and without focus. Armin rubbed his eyes, hoping clarity would be restored. Slowly and with much blinking, an image appeared. It looked like that of a woman dressed in an old-fashioned tunic-style dress. Her waist was cinched tightly with a belt. Tassels hung on either side of her. Over one shoulder was a quiver of arrows; in her hand, she held a crudely made bow. Its size appeared too large for such a slender body. Taking aim, she pulled the string back as far as she could and then opened her fingers, allowing her arrow to fly. The woman's unruly hounds disturbed the serenity of Armin's sanctuary. He recognized the apparition before him, and his laughter echoed, bouncing off the surrounding moss-covered rocks and trees. Calling her name out loud, he beckoned her. "Diana, sister of Apollo, Greek goddess and huntress." Laughing, he looked once again in her direction to see her fade from sight. Lying back, he rested on his elbows drowsily. A book fell from his lap and landed on the soft forest floor. It was titled *Greek Mythology*. That day, Armin's studies suffered, but he didn't care, because he had read the book many times over and knew the lessons it taught. Once again, silence befell the place where he now lay. A sudden snapping of nearby branches brought him back to the present.

Armin's love of nature and its solace would only continue to grow with his age. While lost to the rest of the world, he felt the magnitude of his life with each breath he took. It was as though a million bright lights illuminated his soul. The forest had a knowing of time and spoke its own language. All sounds were hushed as the day's energy shifted to the promise of the setting of the sun and the falling of night. Filled by his experience, he turned, leaving the tranquility of his sanctuary behind. As he emerged from the forest, the shrieking cries of his spirit guide filled the sky above him. Silverhawk glided on the breeze, swooping near him as if to escort him through the meadows, taking him home. The regal bird was not of the earth. It was of God's hands, and guided Armin's every move.

## Chapter Two

# Meeting the Bow

*B*alance and harmony in all things resonated with Armin, and never again did he engage in the discord that often presented itself in daily living. He excelled in academic studies, achieving high grades; yet, he was not a fan of the strict rules and demands put upon him by his teachers and the politics of education. He was disillusioned by those who would insist that he stop dreaming of vocations that would not provide a proper living for him. Professors often accused him of being out of touch with the reality of modern times. They scorned him, as by then, Armin knew far better than they. He believed in himself and knew all things were possible. Desiring freedom from the constrictive institution of academics, he made it his goal to graduate early and succeeded.

During summer holidays, Armin worked as a carpenter, learning plumbing and other building trades, which he did to please his family. Inevitably, he chose to leave, knowing this vocation was not the right path for him. From his early childhood, architecture and drawing were his first loves. Unable to abandon his dreams, he chose to follow his desires, which would ultimately lead to success in his life.

Armin was fifteen years old when he graduated from school. He was anxious to pursue employment in the town where he lived. A small and successful architectural company, which maintained highways and roads in the town of Regensburg, was looking for help. He submitted his résumé and within days received a call to schedule him for an interview with the company's owner. Arriving on time, he showed little external nervousness, realizing this opportunity could be the start of dreams he had always envisioned.

At the main desk, Armin introduced himself to a rosy-cheeked, slightly robust middle-aged woman who found pleasure in eyeing him over her horn-rimmed glasses. Soon, he was escorted to a small conference room where he waited for the company's owner to arrive. Herr Schultz was late but entered the room within half hour of their scheduled appointment. Dressed in a dark-gray suit and wearing a colorful bowtie, he reached out to shake Armin's hand and thanked him for having an interest in the position. Immediately, Armin felt at ease, making the interview process enjoyable. The soft-spoken, kind gentleman exuded fine manners. His demeanor was easy as he asked Armin a cache of questions. Herr Schultz seemed to enjoy talking to Armin and was very satisfied with their meeting. Needing to be elsewhere in the building, Herr Schultz shook hands with the young man, ending their lengthy interview. Armin was confident that he had been well spoken and enthusiastic during their meeting. Sitting for a moment, he sighed and wiped his brow of moisture from his hidden nervousness. Now, he would wait, hoping all would go in his favor.

Herr Schultz was impressed with the young man who seemed to know what he wanted and who had presented himself in a professional way. A week passed before Armin finally received a call from the architectural firm. Schultz had decided to take a chance, offering Armin a position as an apprentice. His generosity was such that Armin could not refuse the position offered him; thus, a new career was born of his desire and positive thinking, proving his notion that he could create the life he wanted with a simple thought.

Matthias Hertzog, a junior partner in the firm, was appointed as Armin's preceptor, helping him to acclimate to the office routine during his first several weeks at work. One day, he noticed that he had forgotten important papers he needed for a project he was working on, Matthias asked Armin if he would accompany him to his home to fetch what he had left behind. It was a warm, sunny day, and Matthias's convertible jeep promised an exhilarating ride. A sense of freedom ran through both of them as the breeze filled their jackets like the luffing sails of a ship flapping in a high wind. They continued on until they finally arrived at Matthias's home. Armin lagged behind as his friend ran inside the house. The house sat on a modest-sized parcel of land with many colorful gardens. The natural scene reminded him of his forest walks, leaving him with a sense of comfort and appreciation.

Raising his eyes, Armin noticed a target at the far end of the garden. Walking toward it, he saw many holes in the bull's-eye. Within minutes, Matthias returned. Looking inquisitively, Armin asked, "Are you an archer?"

"Yes, I am," Matthias replied, "but I haven't shot in some time. Would you like to give it a try?" He then retrieved a bow and some arrows from the shed in the side yard and quickly demonstrated how to use them.

Armin had only seen movies of Robin Hood as a boy, never thinking he would try the sport. Handing Armin a traditional bow and a quiver of arrows, Matthias said, "Here, take them. They have rested for far too long and should be used. Go and have fun with them." Continuing, Matthias told a story of the bow's history. "In China, it is said that when you pluck the bowstring, it releases demons held in the wood. Always remember to respect the bow as if it were alive. Let it rest as you would rest yourself, and it will always perform well for you." Armin took these words and locked them into his mind. Looking in disbelief at the gift he had been given, he gladly took the bow and arrows and studied them. Pulling the string, he listened to the musical rhythm it made. Turning to Matthias, he thanked him and promised to give them great care. Time was passing, and they were late returning to the office. On the ride back to the city, Armin examined the bow's shape, running his hands over the wood. It was smooth with multiple hues of browns and golds. Pulling an arrow from the quiver, he found it to be of light weight, thin, and long. Feathers were strategically placed on one end with a nock (a small cut in the arrow shaft, which nestled the bowstring) while the other end had a pointed metal tip.

Armin's workday was nearly finished, and he was anxious to get home to try out his skills with the bow. Soon he found himself changing out of his work clothes, and then headed to the backyard of his parents' home where he set a bale of hay twenty yards away from where he would begin to shoot. Taking careful aim on the target, Armin immediately liked the feeling of placing the string in the nock and the power in his arms as he drew the arrow back. He felt a swelling in his arms and back muscles with each pull of the bow. Intuitively, he knew the precise moment to release the string and permit the arrow to fly. Somehow, there was a familiarity with the bow, a sense of belonging to it from the very beginning; it was the same as it had been with his love of nature. Each day, he learned more about archery from Matthias, and soon, a great respect and excitement settled in. He knew he would pursue the sport. Armin looked forward to studying the techniques required to master the ancient art form.

Breaking his concentration, a sudden cawing of a bird diverted his attention. Armin's eyes swept the sky. Silverhawk flew downward with great speed close to where he stood. The bird then hovered over him sending a breeze toward his face, moving his hair as if heralding the reawakening of archery and its connection to China, initiating Armin's return home.

Having no one to teach him, Armin would learn on his own. Initially, he had no money available for lessons or to purchase the equipment he needed. Bales of hay would be targets, and his quiver would be the belt on his hips. On his own, he made the best of the situation and practiced day after day for years, never giving up. His body would tire quickly during practice, as happened to anyone trying a new sport that demanded physicality. His arms shook from the tension in his muscles as he increased the draw weight of the bow. Relentlessly, he kept training until he perfected his technique. Youth always brought limited knowledge, yet his continued desire to excel and study opened a new world of ideas, which would be implemented in time to come. He read books on archery and about its masters, always seeking advice from others who had experience in this game, hoping the information provided would improve his skills. During practice, Armin placed his arrow on the string as if placing notes upon a scale. Then, raising his bow hand like the moon rising from his chest, he drew the string back until his middle finger reached the corner of his lip. Looking with two eyes, he found the small spot on the target beyond. He released his arrow, and it sailed before finding its way to the round yellow bull's-eye he had made. Slowly and with great patience, he gained the knowledge he was seeking, learning instinctive shooting. His emptiness of thoughts in coordination with his powerful stance and proper breathing techniques were the keys to perfecting his shot, allowing his intent to take over. It was as though Armin's bow became an extension of his arm.

He was fascinated with the discipline of archery and of Chinese martial arts, particularly of Taijiquan. These exercises were controlled patterns and combinations of flowing movements, each with their own names. These studies demanded concentration and focus, negating all else around him. He was becoming aware of his innermost self. Armin's stance rooted him to the earth as he continued the cycle of breath without pause. The knowledge he gained with his continued determination to learn only improved his skills. Eventually, he was led to understand and implement the philosophy of Dragon and Tiger. The Buddhists called this Chi Kung and the Taoists, Nei Gong. It was the most powerful energy mechanism. It involved a combination of seven body movements cultivating energy flow through the body's outer meridian lines. These bring order, balance, and strength, escalating awareness, sensitivity, and energy flowing throughout the human body, through all of life and matter in the universe. Armin was able to implement this knowledge in conjunction with shooting the bow. As he developed his skills, his proficiency expanded, allowing him to become a master of archery in time. He believed that "you try at nothing; you simply do it." He lived by this motto in all aspects of his life.

Armin was never one to live looking at his past knowing he could not change what was gone, nor did he look too far into the future; instead, he learned to live in the *now*. There were times when his mind would wander out of his control and his thoughts would go back to a past time, perhaps a past life. This he could not help, as often he wondered about the images his mind would see. Dreams and apparitions would slip in and out of his consciousness, negating his control. Armin wondered if he manifested his visions using his theory of positive thinking. Was he calling these entities to him, making them appear? He was uncertain.

In quiet moments, Armin often saw images of a warrior from ancient times. He wondered if it was an ancestor who had returned, one who had come from the Great Republic of China. Again, he was unsure, yet he sat absorbing the visions that came to him and the feelings that shuddered through his body. Armin's dreams were many and changed everything, as each one of them brought a mysterious tale, a new dimension unknown to him. Sadly, the many flashbacks and visions became customary, never allowing him to conclude any truth to the stories of his mind. For many years, these images continued to appear and reappear, yet he never understood what kept them so alive and real. Armin did not resist them; instead, he embraced each one, hoping they would reveal the answer as to why they chose to haunt him.

# Chapter Three
## *Manhood*

The only certain thing in life is that nothing ever remains the same as change is eminent.

---CCC---

*A*rmin's teenage years had flown by, and his responsibilities had grown. Luckily, he had found his way into the business of drawing and architecture and was proud of his career. He had great confidence in the security of his position and was a faithful employee who worked long hours, committed to succeeding and doing well for those who loved and depended on him. He spent weekends with friends and on his continued studies of the martial arts. Taijiquan was now embedded in him, having become a daily practice as with his bow, enabling him to balance his life with ease. Sadly, there was never enough time in Armin's busy life for him to totally immerse himself in all the things he loved to do, those things of great importance to him. His studies of Taijiquan and his way with the bow allowed him a pathway into his own heart and into the richness of the Chinese culture, introducing him to the philosophy of the Tao Te Ching.

In his early twenties, Armin found a new sense of self and purpose; his priorities would change to a more serious state. He had found a special someone; he could not resist the feeling of contentment that love brought. Soon, a new life lay ahead with another by his side. His personal life had taken a slide into the easy comfort of companionship, and all in his world was perfect. Now there were only fleeting gaps of time for him to work with his bow and arrows. Soon, his passion for shooting dwindled lost to the business of his new life.

With many years of expertise behind him, Armin was respected by his peers and those in the company. Herr Raymond Schultz owner of the architectural corporation noticed that the promising man he had taken a chance on years ago had indeed worked very impressively during his long employment at the firm. It was a brisk fall day when Herr Schultz called a meeting of his small office staff. Armin was taken by surprise as Ray Schultz stood before them to make an unexpected announcement. As this was not his usual way, the staff was concerned. Ray was a slim sixty-year-old man in good shape for his age. His white curly hair was receding, and his face was creased with lines carrying worry; still, he was very handsome and spoke with respect to his employees. Silence filled the small conference room as Herr Schultz began to speak. "As you know, the company is doing very well, and I take pride in each of you. However, it seems my years become me. I am tired and in need of a senior partner to share the administrative responsibilities. I have gathered you here to announce my choice for that position. I hope each of you will be cooperative and share with me in welcoming Herr Armin Hirmer."

Stunned, Armin raised his gaze from his hands, which were folded in his lap, wondering at first if he had heard the news correctly. Warmth swept through him, leaving his cheeks a shade of red. Applause and many hands reached out to him in congratulations. He was dazed but stood robotically saying, "Thank you," many times over. His arm was like a rubber toy shaking up and down with each manly grip that met his hand. Office celebrations carried over to his home with friends and family. All were pleased that his ambitions and dreams had come to fruition.

Life from then on brought in substantial financial gains. He was able to buy a home and all the material things that showed the world of his success. He was happy and driven to bring new business to the firm. For years, his life was full and all went exceedingly well.

The Schultz firm had landed a multimillion-dollar contract under Armin's watch, and business was at its peak. Armin was at the pinnacle of his career. Engineers were hired and work crews employed. Carpenters and every trade necessary to start the job were put on the payroll. The project would take years to complete, but they were off and running. The production began without a hitch and the projected completion date seemingly would be met. Ray Schultz, confident in Armin's control of the business, was able to take time off from his grueling schedule frequently. Happily, Armin took charge with pride, knowing his boss trusted him. He assured Herr Schultz that all would go well during his absences.

Nearly two month had passed before Ray returned to work. There was a buzz in the office that perhaps his wife had taken ill. As Ray walked into the firm on a beautiful spring day, he eyed each of his employees, hesitating on each face. With a tilt of his head, he gestured Armin to his office. His coat was buttoned all the way up, protecting him from the cool winds of that early April day; a scarf wrapped around his neck was placed over his mouth. Without a word, Armin followed Herr Schultz into his office, noticing his boss's slow, careful stride. Standing on the far side of Schultz's desk, Armin watched him hang his coat and scarf on the coatrack that stood in the corner of the room near his gray leather chair, which was nestled beneath his desk. Armin observed his every move, immediately noticing upon the removal of his coat that Ray had lost weight. His face was pale and drawn. Armin looked at him questioningly, waiting for words to pour from Ray's mouth. "Sit down," he said in a soft but commanding voice and then continued, "I said nothing earlier because I was unsure of what was going on. Armin, you have been my right-hand man, and I appreciate all that you've done here. Your hard work has been noticed. How old are you now?"

Armin raised his brow and then put his head down, wondering what this had to do with anything. He answered, "Thirty-five."

"Um-hum, a very good age," Schultz said.

Suddenly, sweat began to bead on Armin's forehead as if he were listening to the beginning of a sermon that might end his career. "Is this how someone is fired?" Armin asked under his breath.

Then Herr Shultz spoke again. Armin looked at his lips as they moved in slow motion wondering all the while what was so important. *So what is it?* Armin thought. All had run smoothly during Schultz's extended holiday. What could be wrong? Armin's mind raced. Finally, he took a deep breath and looked up to find a despondent expression on his boss's face.

Herr Schultz stared into Armin's eyes with tears and then just blurted out what he had to say. "I'm very ill, and my time is not long here. I am dying. Armin, I have given this much thought, and I am confident that you can do the job. I am asking you to take over the company. I will help you as best I can—"

Armin interrupted, "But . . . but I thought it was your wife who was ill." Stumbling for words, he simply fell silent.

Herr Schultz continued, "You have been like a son to me and deserve this opportunity. You are the only one I trust."

Shocked, Armin was at a loss, and in his disbelief, he hoped that what he had heard was untrue. Baffled, he continued to watch the words slowly float out of Ray's mouth. Together, they sat, and Ray explained without too much detail that he had a rare and terminal cancer. "A fast mover," he said. They looked at each other in silence, and tears came with ease for both men. Nothing could be said to fill the void of emptiness Armin felt. Promising to take on the responsibility, Armin would lead the team, finish the project at hand, and oversee all other aspects of the company to Ray's satisfaction. They shook hands, and Armin placed his hand on Ray's shoulder like a father to his son, hoping to make things better with a simple touch. With great sadness, he turned and walked away, leaving Ray alone.

Slowly, word of Schultz's illness spread throughout the firm. A state of despair fell over his staff as they wondered about the uncertainty of their own futures. Schultz stayed on at the firm for many months, though he was weak and failing. Four months had passed, and Armin ran the business smoothly, putting in overtime hours to be certain everything was on schedule as he oversaw each detail of the project. As the days passed, Armin noticed the dark circles deepening around Schultz's once sparkling brown eyes. He realized his boss's days were a struggle. He understood Ray didn't want to cave in to his illness; doing so would only be to give up his life. Quite by surprise, a few weeks later, Schultz decided that for whatever time was allotted him, it was best to be with his family. Supporting his decision, Armin promised to check in weekly to keep Shultz informed on the progress being made. He knew that keeping Ray somewhere in the loop would give him purpose, which in truth gave him life.

Nearly eight months had passed since Ray had shared his health issues with Armin. He battled with days of recovery, feeling strong and enjoying remission of his cancer. But still, he chose to stay home, knowing even his good days were riddled with tiredness and bouts of depression. The winter months of cold, snow, and dreary weather played a tug-of-war with his health; his immune system was diminished to nothing, and his battle became futile. There was no more fight left, and he seemed settled in spirit, ready to face the unknown of death. The bleakness of winter had its final way with Herr Schultz, and he succumbed to pneumonia in December just before the Christmas holiday. His life and passing was celebrated with a Holy Mass at St. Peter's Cathedral, one of the most ancient and magnificent gothic architectural sites in Regensburg. There, family and friends would pray for his soul and honor his life and his good deeds. The interment of his body would have to wait for warmer temperatures, when finally the frozen earth would thaw to the yielding promise of spring.

Armin, sorrowful at the loss of Ray, was beginning to feel uncomfortable, as though he was being swallowed by the immensity of his position. He was conflicted between the wanting of material things and his desire for success. Yes, he enjoyed the finer comforts of society that came with his new career, but he had to remind himself that he had always loathed the gluttony of the world. Armin's adult life was going against all that he had believed in in his younger days, having no worth to the man he used to be. He was disappointed in himself, but somehow, he was on a ride that could not stop, being pulled in a direction that did not feel right for him. All of Armin's responsibilities with the architectural firm and the death of Ray Schultz slowly began taking a toll on him. He was bound, as though tied to a chair, having no more sense of freedom. Nighttime would take him to a dark place where at first he would toss and turn, sweat dripping from his face, as rain would fall from the sky. Then he would drift, and his dreams would take him to far-off lands and islands he had never known. There, in his mind, he would sit watching the swells of an ocean wave falling deep into a peaceful state. He stayed as long as his alarm clock would permit. These blissful dreams ended as his new day began. At times, he would feel sick to his stomach, reminding him of his childhood days when school was a burden and he easily manipulated his mind into illness. Life as he had known it was no more, and a change that had occurred deep within him was beginning to surface. He wondered where the simplicity of his life had gone and missed doing what felt right for him.

Now, on his own, Armin took care of the project and other office matters without issue. Digging in deep, he learned to put aside his subconscious mind. He was doing his best to honor his promise to Herr Schultz. Payrolls were met each week on time, and all seemed to be thriving well in Ray's absence. In the eighth week of running the operation alone, Armin was approached by many angry employees complaining that their checks had bounced. He was bombarded with complaints by those working on the project outside the office as well. Armin's mind was swirling in disbelief, unable to understand what had gone so very wrong. Immediately, he visited the bank trying to find out what had happened. He was certain there was a glitch in the programming at the bank. The International Bank of Germany was huge, handling corporate businesses by the thousands. Armin found himself in a large plush office leaning back in a big leather chair. He sat waiting for the supervisor to return so he could report the problems he was having with the financial accounts for Schultz Architectural. Soon, Herr Hess arrived and listened attentively as Armin detailed his story. The well-groomed gentleman stood and then left the office, explaining he would return with an answer. Forty-five minutes had passed before the supervisor Herr Hess took his place in front of Armin once again. Pacing the floor, Armin turned. With a look of embarrassment on his face, Herr Hess stumbled for words at first. His face grew red, and he coughed several times as if to clear his throat and then spoke with confidence. "I am so sorry, Herr Hirmer. I don't quite know how to say this to you, but it seems that with the death of Herr Schultz came the death of all the finances. Sir, all the accounts have been frozen."

Armin's heart sank. *How could this happen? I have no way to pay any of the staff.* Looking at the supervisor for more information, he felt panic set in. Herr Hess then explained that no legal documents had been filed placing Armin's name on any of the accounts. Armin then realized that the promised transactions, those that would have made him a senior partner in the firm had never been signed, as he was promised. It was a nightmare of great magnitude, one that would set the stage for the failure of Schultz Architectural unless a miracle happened.

Immediately, Armin retained a lawyer to counsel him on what would come next. For nearly a year, Armin worked with creditors trying to find a resolve, one which would keep the firm afloat. His efforts were to no avail. He was being pursued by legal actions inferring he was personally responsible for the failings of the company. Millions of dollars in debt, Armin knew there was no way out. Eventually, a settlement satisfying the creditors alleviated him of personal responsibility. In the meantime, his peers had found new positions elsewhere and some of his friends had turned their backs on him, leaving Armin to wonder if they were ever true friends at all. By this time, his life as it had been was no more, his reputation was in question, and his personal life in all aspects was nonexistent. The happy family life he had known also ended sadly in divorce. His life was in ruins!

Armin found himself accepting emptiness. Alone, he took only a few belongings with him and walked away from his life, his home, and those he loved, knowing all the while that the failure of Schultz Architectural was in no way his fault. It was the fault of Schultz himself, an ill man, whose concerns were for his own health, family, and the preservation of what life he had left. The firm was an appendage of his stellar days, something that no longer served him and was not a viable part of his struggles ahead. Ray never said a formal good-bye to anyone and seemingly turned away, forgetting all those who had considered themselves a part of his family. Many had spent a lifetime in service to him. Silently, Ray simply packed his office, turned his back, and walked out the door, never looking back. Perhaps his sorrow would not let him leave any differently. Armin was not shocked; he realized that although Ray appeared to be in control, accepting his illness and fate to come, in truth, he was sadly caught in a whirlwind of panic and confusion. Armin would not permit himself to dwell on these circumstances. There was no point; it was over, and he chose not to look back. Never did he carry anger for the plight now ahead of him. Instead, he remembered a time before when he put his faith in knowing there was a purpose in all that happened, a lesson to be learned. As harsh and destructive as this one was in all aspects of his life, he chose to believe that some good would come out of this misery.

Armin was in need of rebirth, and he fondly remembered the simplicity of the life he had once known. He relished each thought, knowing his recovery would allow him a new sense of freedom. For too many years, he had been pulled away from his source by the many obstacles life put before him. Caught up in the mental realm of everyday living, he was torn and empty, walking forward into uncertainty. His spirituality had dulled, and he longed to find all that seemed to be missing, replacing the many years when turmoil had taken him over. His bow had slept far too long and the simplicity of his life gone. Armin now often reflected back to his childhood when he would retreat to the solitude of the forest. These thoughts were pleasing. He remembered the simple perfection of peaceful, uncomplicated days lost in time. He promised to renew his way of life and his spirituality, for each longed to be reawakened. There would be no more routines to follow, leaving him an open path to the future. He did not fully understand the subtle stirring within him, nor could he ignore the pulling he felt. Immediately, Armin began turning his life into a place of comfort, which he had shut out for far too long. The bow fever that had stolen his soul as a young man was the answer to finding harmony in his life. With his past responsibilities behind him, Armin diverted his attention to those things now of greater importance.

Designed by Armin Hirmer

## Chapter Four

# The Art of Taijiquan

*T*aijiquan enabled Armin to find his center and focus. He maintained an absolute state of relaxation, and graceful sequential movements cultivated his complete body power, allowing chi energy to flow throughout his entire body. Gratified, he felt a newness swell within him and the emergence of peace, and an excitement for all that awaited was born. Armin was seeking to understand the riddles of life and to reconnect with his Source, with the heavens and the universe. These disciplines taught him better health. He ate only in moderation and only the things needed to sustain himself in a natural way. There would be no gluttony of any kind. Neither alcohol nor drugs were ever a part of him at any time. He promised himself that nothing of his past life would come into the present. Connected now with his body, mind, and spirit, Armin became more aware of the conscious choices that he made during his daily life, allowing him to obtain oneness of self.

There would be times of clashing when his two worlds made no sense. During these moments of wonder, Armin would go stand on the bridge over the Danube River in Regensburg, where he always felt a peaceful connection with all of nature. He loved to watch the setting of the sun from this place while listening to the water splashing on the walls along the riverbanks below. Melting as one with the painted scene in front of him, he was confident that the days to follow would be filled with a new hope and understanding. Armin's thoughts were like a mist slowly rising from the river below him, riding on a silent breeze as it moved up along the mountain side, sailing off into oblivion. The shrilling whistle of Silverhawk awakened him from his musings. Looking toward the sky, the white tips of the great bird's wings passed near as it circled in flight as if to tell his story. In that very moment, he made the decision to follow his heart, move forward alone with confidence, and leave behind the country of his birth. The presence of Silverhawk was inspiring. Armin's purpose was suddenly clear. It seemed that words were being given to him by his spirit guide, prodding him in a new direction. It was saying, "You are the Archer. Go teach. For when one teaches, two will learn. It is said that the archer must have stillness, grace, and poise, becoming one with the bow as his energy merges with its soul and spirit." Armin had already infused this knowledge into his daily living and the use of his bow. It was now time to offer all he had to those who would listen.

# Chapter Five

# Wudang

"Me, Myself, and I."

*D*uring his first twenty years of practicing archery, Armin used the Mediterranean style of shooting, which required three fingers on the string when pulling it back. As his skills matured, he was introduced to the Asian style of shooting, engaging only the thumb to draw the string, with the index finger over it and the rest of the fingers clinched. From the very first shot he made using this technique, he felt comfortable. It seemed to be a natural way of shooting for him. His body was in perfect alignment to make his shot. First, he widened his feet to be directly under his shoulders, balancing his weight between them, his knees slightly bent as his hips were rotated to flatten the small of his back. Armin centered himself then, focused on his breathing, which remained natural as he drew air in through his nose and exhaled in the same manner. He continued the even cycle of breathing, moving air easily in and out of his lungs. Aware at first of his stance, grounding himself to the earth, Armin then emptied his mind of all thoughts, permitting the arrow to find its intended mark once released. Often, while practicing, he would see images before him, images he could not explain. At first, he wondered if it was the velocity of the arrow in flight that vibrated the energy around him, bringing faded visions and melodic sounds swirling into focus. Loosening his grip on the bow, Armin let it rest by his side, allowing this energy to have its way with him. His study of martial arts had taken root in him in ways that could not be described. He noticed that his sensitivities were heightened and his intuition was now beyond even his understanding.

Eric Klinger, a student in Taijiquan, was a friend with whom Armin had studied in Germany. Armin's mastership of the martial arts and learning of the tea ceremony were becoming second nature, a part of him. They were ingrained in his soul. Eric had noticed growth and significant developments in Armin's life since he had chosen to return to his core being. Knowing of the passion that lay within Armin and his thirst for knowledge, Eric felt it was time to share all he had experienced, things which had brought him total peace in his own life. One evening, while at dinner, Eric's girlfriend, who was a native of China, shared the stories and myths pertaining to the mysteries of the Fairy Mountains of Wudang, China. The many stories they both told gave Armin a view of a very different way of life, one he needed to know on a more personal level. Realizing that storytelling and pictures of Wudang were not enough, he meditated and set Wu Wei in place (action by no action). His desire to feel and experience the mystery of Wudang's spirituality was simply far too great to ignore. Armin knew that a visit to Wudang would assist him in finding his true source and light, beginning the ultimate completion of his soul's journey.

Everything is energy,
And that's all there is to it.
Match the frequency
of the reality you want,
And you cannot help
But get that reality.
It can be no other way.
This is not philosophy.
It is physics.

—Albert Einstein

Months had passed and thoughts of Wudang grew daily as Armin prepared for one of the most insightful journeys of his lifetime. He would begin the first leg of his travel at Munich International Airport with one small bag. He stood in a long line of passengers waiting to board his plane. In twelve hours, he would find himself standing on Chinese soil, a land full of rich tradition and culture. He would feel the spirituality that swept the atmosphere as the peaked mountains touched the sky. There, he would learn various forms of martial arts as well as sword dancing and pushing hands. He would engage in the deepest form of meditation, allowing him counsel with his soul and oneness with the universe. Armin would teach his way with the bow and even share his knowledge of the Chinese tea ceremony. He projected that his journey would go smoothly, and excitement swelled in him as his plane landed. Buses and taxis awaited the many passengers ready to take them to their destinations. Within several days of his arrival, Armin finally made his way to Wudang.

He was met by many monks (Monachos), whose order came of Christian origin centuries ago. They were also influenced at that time by the Orthodox Greek religion and customs. These Buddhist monks were like Catholic bishops or priests, men who had chosen to live their lives in contemplation and prayer. They lived in harmony with the Tao, which was, "the way, path, or principle," denoting both the driving force and source of everything that exists. From the Tao Te Ching, written by Lao Tzu, Armin learned the foundation of philosophy representing Taoism. Other masters, such as Zhuangzi, were also influential in his studies. He did not consider Taoism a religion of organization but instead a host of integrated concepts of yin and yang and of naturalism and the five elements. He learned that Taoist ethics varied but emphasized Wu Wei (action by no action), meaning naturalness, spontaneity, and simplicity in life, in essence permitting the universe to have its own way. Beyond these, he learned of the three treasures: moderation, humility, and the greatest of these, which led to the ultimate way of the Tao, compassion. Armin had always lived "the way," from his very first days as a child. Being connected to a higher source, he often wondered from where this had come.

In the beginning was the Tao.
All things issue from it
All things return to it.
To find the origin,
Trace back the manifestations.
When you recognize the children

And find the mother,
You will be free of sorrow.
Close your mind in judgments
And traffic with desires,
Your heart will be troubled.
If you keep your mind from judging
And aren't led by the senses,
You will find peace.
Seeing into darkness is clarity.
Knowing how to yield is strength.
Use your own light
And return to the source of light.
This is called practicing eternity.

—#52 (Tao Te Ching), Lao Tzu

Spending his first night in the city below the mountains, Armin recognized that the ancient ways of China seemed lost in a new and modern era, making it clear to him that the world of technology and computers had now reached it fingers out to the entire world, putting each of us within a communicable moment of time with one another. City traffic was busy, bringing the chaos of tooting horns and blaring radios and offering nothing of a peaceful, mysterious, or spiritual ambiance. The static energy became frenzied to him, disturbing his natural sense of harmony. This energy changed the faces of society, making it nearly impossible for humans to look one another in the eye and communicate. Even more, he saw that humanity was becoming a zombie-like society where imaginations and creativity were stagnant. Simple living was well on its way to extinction. Armin found these truths to be offensive and was saddened to realize that humankind was losing itself. He hoped that people would open themselves up, becoming aware that they were not only observers of life but were also observed by the entire universe. Humankind was failing to see the truth within the word *existence*. Armin realized beyond all others that we are but a speck of dust floating within the cosmos, one with all that is, sending energy for the good of the universe. Each living soul is on its own journey and must live fully following his or her heart.

Photo by Armin Hirmer

Traveling many long hours up the long, winding trails, which led high into a range of jagged peaks, Armin began to notice a shift in the air. A presence enfolded him, sending chills up his spine, leaving him with a feeling he could not explain. The skies were clear, and the herbal fragrances he smelled were pure and clean. The mountain winds of Wudang sang the glory of a higher spirit, of one who danced among the temples and who lived in this place above the noises of the civilized world. Peace and love held the intentions of good and of God, which filled the atmosphere, capturing the multitudes of pilgrims who came to visit each year. Wudang Mountain, located in China's Northern Hubei Province, was constructed sometime in the seventh century BC and was regarded as the Fairy Mountains and a sacred land of Chinese Taoism (Daoism). It had a mystical charm and appeal, which called to the hearts of many; it was a setting of natural beauty and home to the Temples of Heaven. The buildings that graced these mountains were built by the Tang and Ming Dynasties centuries earlier. They embodied a mysterious magic and divine light that captured souls. Armin loved places of simplicity and beauty, ever void of the ego mind. It offered a purity that permitted him to reach oneness with the universe. This, he found difficult to replicate while living within the confusion and noise of a modern society. There among the holy mountain temples and monks, he felt a profound sense of himself. He did not speak Chinese, yet he was able to communicate with the monks and others who knew through intuition and hand motions what his needs were. Armin made a profound spiritual connection that would embed itself in his core, changing his life forever. The knowledge he gained was a perfection of self-study and of discipline, all of which he used to further perfect his life and archery techniques. He reaffirmed the importance of living in the now, insisting that the very moment presenting itself was all there truly was, and it was so. Sitting atop the world, Armin would empty his mind of all thought as he had always done in shooting the bow; there, silence prevailed, and he easily drifted into blankness, where he heard the voice of God.

Over the months that followed, he was content in a way he had never truly known. His days were filled with new friends as he learned of the traditions of the mountain people, opening yet another new pathway in his life. Each day brought a new experience, a depth in learning of push-hand and self-defense maneuvers and a true meaning of meditation. Here, he learned that to sit or even to stand with oneself and meditate is not only to escape the chaos and stress of the world but to reach a place of inner peace and serenity. Sitting empty-minded, he could enter into the spaces between his thoughts. In accordance with the wisdom traditions, these spaces between thoughts were a window, a corridor, and the vortex to the infinite mind. It was the place where God and spirit dwelled. It was the core conscientiousness, a place where one observed and implemented the power of intention. This void between thought evoked infinite possibilities and pure potential, igniting imagination and creativity. Here, Armin came to understand that all things were connected.

Sadly, his time on the Mountain of Wudang was coming to an end. He tried to refute the reality of his impending departure, wanting to stay forever in the paradise he had found. Yet fate would have its way with him, and in this, he had no say. In the last days before Armin's departure, he felt the need to fill himself with the purity of the air that filled the atmosphere on the highest peaks, for it brought a euphoria heightening his chi, allowing him to flow again not as an observer but as one with the universe. With each breath he took, he would feel himself levitate and leave the earthly world, finding his place with God. The monks in the lower mountains would ask the elders of his whereabouts; they simply looked at one another and smiled as they turned a finger to the highest peak, knowing he was there.

Photo by Armin Hirmer

## Chapter Six

# Descending the Mountain

*A*rmin sat beneath a four-hundred-year-old tree, which shaded him from the sun's rays. Fragrant aromas from six hundred indigenous herbs, which grew throughout the lower woodlands, danced up the mountainside. There, he meditated for days, asking of his place in life and direction for his soul's purpose. It was the fourth day upon the mountain when the once-clear blue sky scattered with wisps of soft floating mist became obscured by billowing cumulous clouds readying to burst with tears. A sudden stir in the wind found Armin unprepared for the change of color to ominous hues of charcoal gray. The wind began to come at him with a forceful punch. A crack of lightning blinded him momentarily, and his heartbeat was rapid as fear struck like a sword. His rational mind told him that all was well, yet the sky continued to darken. Thunder roared from the heavens, echoing across the lower valley, shaking the mountain to its highest point. The storm rolled over him, fast and furious. Lightning continued to crack through the sky, like a charioteer's whip. He was caught in the drenching downpour, as the mountain relentlessly shook beneath him. Armin was humbled in the presence of Mother Earth and the power she so easily unleashed, knowing he was no match for this storm of such might. Blindly, he reached his arm out into the darkness, searching for something to hold on to, so that he might steady himself against the forceful wind that moved him, like a branch of a tree. His hand held tight to the narrow limb for support. He hoped the storm would leave as quickly as it had come. Suddenly, another burst of wind sent Armin's feet out from beneath him, and the narrow limb gave way, sending him to the ground. Soon enough, the storm clouds swept over the mountain, bringing calm, which allowed him to catch his breath and wipe his face and hair. He had been drenched with the soaking rain. Still holding tight to the wood, he brought it nearer to his eyes. Perplexed by what he saw, he recognized a golden arrow, gleaming even in the darkness of the storm. Disbelief overtook him, he examined every inch of the arrow, finding beneath its soaked feathers something carved lightly on it. Squinting to read the message, he treasured its words. He found himself repeating its phrase over and over. *"You have found your way."* Not fully understanding the meaning, Armin knew that time would help him solve the riddle of the arrow.

He turned to walk the path down the hillside. A sudden thick mist swirled around him as if the winds were teasing him once again. In his weakened, bewildered state, Armin was easily pushed from side to side like a sail luffing on rough waters stirred by a raging storm. Hesitating for a moment, he tried to get his bearings but recognized nothing. Certain it would be only moments until the fog lifted, he waited patiently. Soon, the roar of the wind blew away any remnants of the storm.

Before him was a pathway lined with trees that towered above him. It hadn't been there before, yet it seemed to offer safe passage off the mountain, promising protection from any lingering rainfall or relentless rays from the emergence of the sun. Armin did not question what was before him. He willingly walked the path that offered a way back to civilization—or so he hoped. Often, he would check his bearings, turning in each direction, looking for something familiar. Yet the area he had known so well was unrecognizable. He was lost!

In the confusion of the storm, Armin realized he had left his bow and arrows behind. He was certain they too had been blown about like twigs or fallen leaves before being hurled into space, pulled into a funnel of powerful wind, and dispersed to the heavens, as he nearly was. They had become a part of his daily dress, and he felt naked without them at his side. Desperate to feel comfortable, he looked among the branches that had fallen in the storm, trying to find a piece of wood to shave into, at least, a bow for his use. There was nothing adequate to be found. He shook his head knowing that his ego mind was speaking but without foundation, so he let all thought go, trusting in the universe and God's hand.

Armin knew it was best to change his focus, allowing all to unfold naturally. He had traveled since morning, and the day would soon find its end. Lost in the density of the vast forest with its meandering trails, he hoped that one would reveal itself, but it was not to be. Ambling on, he looked for signs of a small village nearby, yet there was nothing, not even the sounds of bells, birds, or the human voice were to be heard. He was lost! Soon, darkness would begin to creep in, obscuring his way. His stomach gnawed as hunger overtook him. He remembered the only food he had eaten was in the early morning hours. Stumbling upon a small lake fed by mountain streams, he quenched his thirst with pure, clean water. Low bushes filled with berries gave him sustenance, enough to carry him on his way. He was thankful that the universe had answered his silent wish.

Finding shelter for the night was paramount. If need be, he would build a lean-to, which would get him through until morning. Continuing on his way, Armin meditated, visualizing his needs once more. He thought of a place where he could find warmth in the cold night and food to satisfy his hunger. Taking a moment, he closed his eyes and sent his thoughts out to the heavens, much like the release of his arrow, knowing all would be as God intended. After many more miles of hiking through thick brush and towering groves of trees, Armin saw a light beyond coming from a small house with a thatched roofed. Covered with moss and vines on the north side, it appeared to be well kept. Plumes of billowing gray smoke spewed from the chimney as welcoming smells of burning firewood filled the air. The house stood alone, set in a time warp. It was from centuries ago with no other neighbors in sight. Cautiously, Armin approached the entrance and knocked on the door, but no one answered. Stepping out from the cover of the makeshift porch roof, he scanned the grounds for someone who lived there.

Silverhawk's piercing cries broke the silence of the forest. Appearing, as if from nowhere, the great bird dived at his head. Armin pulled back to miss the clutch of his talons, setting him off balance. In doing so, he missed being hit by an arrow. Instinctively, he turned to its source, finding a man with a bow and arrow in hand pointing it straight at him. The man before him was dressed in dark clothing of Mandarin style, his face stern yet handsome. Still in control of the situation, the man directed Armin with the tip of his arrow, gesturing for him to step back away from the house. He looked upon Armin with fire in his eyes, as would any man protecting his property. His jet-black hair was slicked back away from his face, held tight with a rawhide string, which allowed his hair to remain draped over his right shoulder. Armin was alarmed that this man would take such a serious action against him, yet he understood the need to protect his property. The man's voice was strong and commanding. Bits of English mixed with a Chinese dialect unfamiliar to Armin. The man holding the bow asked him what he was doing in the middle of the forest so far from civilization. Armin tried to explain calmly with the few Chinese words he knew, telling the man what had happened on the high mountain and of the storm that had left him unsure of his whereabouts. The man looked confused, not understanding the words of explanation.

Within moments, five humble words changed everything. Placing his hands on his chest, Armin said, "I am called 'the Archer.'" Motioning with his hands, he continued, "I have come here from Europe to learn the secrets of the sacred mountains and to share what knowledge I have."

Seeming to understand, the man bowed, apologizing for his harsh behavior. He then smiled and introduced himself as though his actions were forgotten.

"Hai," the farmer said as he in turn tapped his hands on his chest. "I am the bow maker on the mountain, and I have heard of your visit here. You are the one who travels with Silverhawk." Armin looked at Hai, not understanding any of his rambling except for the word *Silverhawk* and only then, because Hai pointed toward the sky. They both smiled and bowed from the waist as Hai called for his wife, Lihua; their daughter, Meifeng; and their son, Bolin, to come meet this visitor of reputation. From a small thicket of brush, they came forward shyly, nodding their heads as they passed before the Archer. Hai then motioned all into the house where Lihua made tea. The men talked as best they could, given their language barrier.

Hai noticed Armin carried no bow or set of arrows. Not wanting to insult or embarrass his guest, Hai asked with wonder how this could be. "You are the Archer. Why is it that you have no tools at your disposal?" He motioned Armin to a rear door off the small kitchen, and together, they made their way to a covered workshop just outside the main house. In front of them stood a long table where

Hai crafted bows and arrows for businesses down the mountain. Hai did not say anything of this to the Archer and only motioned him to help himself in making a new bow and set of arrows. The men worked side by side, without words, long into the evening. A sense of comfort and trust fell upon them, as each was pleased with his new acquaintance. From time to time, Hai glanced at the Archer's eyes, trying to get a glimpse into his soul, but Armin would never permit such intimacy, so they simply nodded and turned back to work.

Hai was very particular with the materials he used and stocked many different types of wood, exactly the same as those preferred by the Archer. Lifting the wood to his nose, Armin smelled its sweetness, appreciating the earth it came from. For his choosing, there were yew and hickory, which were typically used for the traditional Western-style longbows. The bow he had lost was made from bamboo. Somehow, Hai had all of them there in his simple yet well-equipped workshop. Armin tried to communicate with Hai with hand motions and broken Chinese, asking why he had so many materials for bow making in the middle of the forest so far from life. Hai explained that he was commissioned to make these bows of different styles and wood for others in the villages below the mountain.

Turning away, Hai pulled a picture from the wall cabinet. It was a photo with tattered edges. It seemed to have been taken long ago. Hai's ancestor, dressed in traditional Chinese attire made from colorful silks laced with golden thread, stood out from the others. Hai smiled as his finger tapped on the man in the photo, assuring Armin that he who was dressed in such fine clothing was indeed his great-great-uncle, who was a well-known archer of long ago. He had a reputation for great skill and strength and taught the emperor's army to fight using bows and arrows during times of conflict. It was said that he and the emperor became friends and his uncle would often visit the royal palace. Hai raised his brow as he smiled, looking at Armin and said, "He too lived by the bow." It was this uncle who had passed down the skills of archery to all the generations that followed. Armin felt a kinship with Hai's story, knowing he was in a place of great history and truth, not only in the making of the bow but of the respect it was shown. He smiled at Hai, understanding all he had said.

Turning his focus back to the work table, Armin began to his craft his new bow by choosing a sturdy piece of wood. He made the center limb of bamboo, while the handle and the siyah's he made from hardwood. The belly or inside he layered with water buffalo horn, and the back or outside of the bow was layered with sinew. This would be his new composite bow. Armin specifically designed the new bow to fit his draw length, the distance between the throat of the grip to the nock point at the end of a fully drawn arrow plus approximately one to two inches. His desired draw weight was the peak amount of weight pulled when drawing the bow. Within days, his bow, which usually took many weeks or even years to craft properly, would soon be ready for use. His attention then turned to making his new arrows. Hai had cedar, bamboo, and river cane, all of which were at Armin's fingertips. He chose only hardwood for his arrows. Making certain to sharpen both ends like a pencil, he placed glue on one end with a nock. On the other end, he put a sharp metal tip. The feathers he cut in traditional shapes and lengths. Armin's preference was gray goose feathers in five-inch lengths.

**First Night**

At evening's end, both men were tired and in need of a good, long rest. Hai guided Armin to a small room off the work area where he would spend the night. The room was less than modest, but he appreciated the kindness of the family. Feelings of gratitude shot through him like an arrow. With a soft smile and nod from each, the two bowed in respect. Hai closed the door behind him and then abruptly opened it with a large grin on his face, startling Armin. With broken English, he asked the Archer if he would be willing to show all his family how to shoot. Hai recognized the Archer's mastery and knew that skillfully taught lessons would be invaluable. Pleased with his request, Armin nodded his head, agreeing to the task. For how else could he repay Hai's kindness, if not with the teaching of his way with the bow?

Safe from the forest nightlife, Armin placed his head on a soft pillow made of sweet grass covered with a silk pillow case. Then, he wrapped himself with a thick, soft blanket in shades of gray and black with hand-sewn stitches of red thread running through its hems. The blanket had been placed at the foot of the bed earlier by Lihua, Hai's wife, knowing full well that her husband would extend an invitation for the Archer to stay as long as he would like.

Armin had always chosen to live in the now, knowing it would bring all God intended and leave behind that which no longer served him. Comfortable and exhausted, he lay back, thinking of the lightning storm that came so suddenly upon him, stunning his body and disorienting him enough that he was unable to find his way. Bewildered by the events of the day, he stood firm in knowing that all things had a purpose and, in time, he would realize the lesson in this turn of events. His eyes fluttered momentarily, and his breathing slowed as he drifted off into the depths of silence.

Armin happily met the morning, feeling rested and looking forward to teaching. Stepping from his tiny room, he was met with enthusiasm by Meifeng and Bolin. The previous night, the two had said nothing and only stared with wonder at the stranger with blond hair and eyes of changing blue like the sky. This morning, for some unknown reason, their timidity had disappeared. Taking Armin's hands, they led him into the small eating place where Lihua set out a simple breakfast of homemade breads, nuts, and berries. After eating, the children stood watching anxiously, waiting for the Archer to take his last sip of tea before pulling him from the table. Armin was amused by their silent antics and looked each in the eye, summing them up. He surmised that Meifeng was twelve years old.

She was a quiet observer, reminding Armin of himself in his earlier days. Shyly, Meifeng held her gaze toward the floor and only dared from time to time to look over her brow and meet his intense but kind eyes. She would be a beauty in time. She had perfect milky skin and long black hair, which covered her like a silk scarf that flowed down her back. Her cheekbones were high, bringing attention to her large, almond-shaped brown eyes. Armin noticed they carried within them the reflection of an old and very wise soul. She was gentle, polite, and caring to the stranger before her. Meifeng's brother, Bolin, was younger, perhaps ten, but that was only a guess. He was short of stature with a hint of weight, which his youthful body still held onto with grace. Bolin's bright eyes would crinkle as laughter filled him, hinting at a bit of mischief, which radiated from his illuminating smile. Armin found his giggles infectious. A stern look from his mother reminded him of his proper place with the stranger. Realizing his excitement needed to be curbed; Bolin placed his chubby little hands over his mouth to hide his wide smile. Sheepishly, he looked to the Archer for approval. Armin could only smile, knowing full well the feelings of both the children. He was grateful for the gestures they shared with him.

Noticing that Armin had finished his tea, Meifeng and Bolin took the Archer by his hands and led him outside. Leaning his body back toward Lihua, he thanked her for the breakfast. His eyes questioned the whereabouts of Hai; with a simple smile, she pointed to the field beyond the far side of the house. The children spoke to one another in excited tones, and somehow, the Archer understood the conversation and felt their excitement. He watched their dancing eyes and hand gestures as they tugged him along. After passing through the second field and a thicket of trees, they came upon a larger field of low-cut grass with a large group of people waiting with great anticipation. Each stared at the man being led into their midst. Armin noticed they had brought their own bows. They were small, many crudely made, and of various styles. Their arrows were in an array of sizes, many with missing feathers.

Once released by the children, Armin's stride was even and steady. He walked with the grace of a leopard, surefooted and regal. His posture was straight, suggesting confidence and great strength, yet his manner was gentle and smile inviting. The group watched as the stranger approached them and wondered about his skills, ones they had never been able to achieve. What was his secret? Was it the same secret that their ancestors possessed? Armin found Hai among the people and asked where so many had come from. Hai explained, "Many eyes watched you as you descended the mountain. You were never alone on the path." Then spreading his arms out toward the others, he introduced the stranger. "This is my family!"

The Archer laughed. "So many?" he questioned. Armin studied each face before him, feeling comfortable with the task at hand; knowing each of them would have enough knowledge to become masterful at shooting the bow once he had finished teaching them.

A light murmur stirred the silence of the morning. Suddenly, from nowhere, the swishing of an arrow in flight soared inches above their heads. The arrow met the edge of the target at the far end of the field. Piercing screams from Silverhawk and his frantic patterns of flight brought all eyes toward the heavens. The whispers were no more, as all looked with fear toward the sky, watching the flight of Silverhawk, as if they followed a rainbow to its end.

Gazing with great confidence and a grin from ear to ear, Zu-Ling Choi stood high on a hill at the edge of the forest where uneven mounds of earth met with the flat field on which the others stood. He was proud to have created a disturbance, instilling fear in the minds of his own family. What he thought to be a gesture of strength was nothing less than a display of thoughtless arrogance and indignation. Hai raised his voice in reprimand as the young man ignored the dismay of all who gazed at him. His smug attitude was one that needed to be reined in. Zu-Ling was the fourth-generation wayward nephew of Hai's famous ancestral uncle, Qin Li. Zu-Ling believed that his ancestor's spirit walked within him. It was youthful arrogance that drove him to careless measures to prove his strength and prowess as an archer. All were displeased with the disrespect he had shown their visitor, yet Armin did not judge him. He did not display anger or fear; instead, he felt compassion.

The two men came face-to-face. Unimpressed, the Archer guided the young man to the shooting field. Hai's nephew looked up at the foreigner. After studying his face, he looked deep into his eyes. Without words, he walked behind Armin and found his way to the proper distance from the target. As Armin passed Zu-Ling's family, he stopped for a moment and said, "Do not be filled with fear. Remember always, that life begins where fear ends. He will learn."

Flippantly, Zu-Ling raised his bow and shot. His arrow veered off, missing the target entirely. Trying again, he gave more thought to his next attempt. This time, the arrow met the targets outside edge. All eyes were fixed on the two men. The Archer remained composed without any expression. Again, their eyes met, but this time, Zu-Ling felt blood surge through his body. Embarrassment and humiliation swept through him as his extended family looked on. Sweat began pouring from his brow as his own negative energy swirled around him. Still, he pulled an arrow from the quiver, aimed, and met failure once more. His almond-shaped eyes now squinted to only a thin line as he tried harder to find the mark beyond. Without any more words, Armin took up his bow, raising it enough to find the mark, emptying all thoughts from his mind. He drew the string back effortlessly, simultaneously exhaling and holding his breath until his release and follow-through were complete. Silencing his breath, he hit the target with perfection. Zu-Ling wondered about the Archer and then angrily tried again as agitation filled his mind.

"Who is this man to humiliate me in front of my own?" Zu-Ling exclaimed in a loud voice. His face turned red with anger; his heart raced out of control.

Calmly, Armin studied the young man knowing of his profound insecurity from his complicated body language. Turning toward him, Armin said, "It is your ego-mind that is in your way. Empty it! You are one of many and each is the same, no better, no worse. Once you have the target in focus, set your intention aside. The arrow will find its way home."

Zu-Ling studied the Archer's face, looking for signs of judgment, but he found none. The Archer then placed his hand on the young man's shoulder. At first, he pulled back, resisting the gesture, but a sudden calm came over him, as if magic settled his unrest. Armin then said, "Relax, breathe deeply, and focus at first on the target and then on nothing. Let your thought go; rely only on your intent. You have nothing to prove to me or to anyone. You only have to satisfy yourself, so do it! It will do you good to sit in silence and think of who you are and who you want to become. Each can change if he has the desire to do so. Becoming the warrior does not take strength but attitude and commitment. It does not mean you must fight the world. Instead, it means you must have honor and integrity and live by a standard of goodness under the laws of nature and the universe. Come; I will show you the way I use."

Zu-Ling took his position in front of Armin, feeling all eyes upon him. "Stand centered on the ground. Put equal weight on both your feet. Now gently bend your knees. Think from the ground upward and relax. Rotate your hips. Straighten your spine to the top of your head.

Shoulders are relaxed." Armin placed his hand on one of Zu-Ling's shoulders and pushed it down into a more relaxed position, showing him a better way. "Empty your mind as you breathe in through your nose, pulling the air deep inside. Let your belly relax outward. Now gently blow the air out the same way it entered. Continue this practice for several moments, relaxed and easy."

Armin then turned his attention to the rest of the family as they waited patiently for their turn with him. Their eyes showed they were happy that someone had chosen to stand firm against the young man who so needed guidance. Armin understood Zu-Ling's need for kindness, love, and direction in his life.

Hai, with some of the others, went ahead and set up several more targets so they could all shoot at the same time. Armin was pleased by this and began with the basic techniques, as he had with Zu-Ling, who continued the pattern on his own. First, Armin instructed them in how to stand in a relaxed way, beginning with the foot. He taught them to bend their knees slightly, rotate the pelvis, and work their way up the body. Once the core was set, breathing techniques were implemented to relax the archers. He taught them how to hold the bow, finding comfort with it as they ran their hands along the wood, following its curves. The Archer then asked them to pluck the string, much the same as he had done in his youth. Each could feel the spirit of the wood. In a voice no louder than a whisper, he brought all eyes upon himself, saying, "Always use your bow and arrows with safety in mind. For the bow lives and must be cared for properly. Allow it to rest, and in all things, remember to respect both of them." Armin's words were the same as those Matthias had spoken years before.

Soon, young and old alike were taking their turns finding some success hitting the target while others struggled. Each student was like a newborn child under the watchful eye of a father. Armin knew who needed more guidance just by looking. He could tell by the way they stood or carried themselves, assessing their personalities and characters easily. Now and again, his eyes would look to Zu-Ling, who had become more thoughtful as he listened to the Archer instructing the others. Attempting to release his ego mind, he found improvement. As the hours passed, Armin still had concern for Zu-Ling, knowing that time would provide a better understanding of all he was learning. Several times during the day, they walked and spoke at great length. Eventually, Zu-Ling softened, letting down his guard, accepting the Archer's guidance.

Late in the day, Armin ended the lessons by telling Hai's family that he would return the next day for those interested in continuing to learn his way of the bow. Elated, they bowed in appreciation and respect. Quickly, they all went on their way. The Archer returned with Hai and his family for a satisfying supper and another night in the small room off the workshop.

**Nightfall**

Later that night, Armin lay thinking about the day and felt peaceful, knowing each member of Hai's family had learned one thing they had not known the day before. He smiled when thinking of Hai's twin sisters, Qing and Hung. Qing was thin and shy. She was certainly timid by all accounts, having no particular athletic prowess. Each time she pulled the bowstring, she would let out a strange noise as if in anguished pain. Her face contorted like a rubber band when pulling the bowstring and not once did she hit the target. On the other hand, her sister Hung was taller and stronger. She had an open and verbal way about her. She learned quickly all she was taught, having no problem meeting the target with each shot. Every now and again, she directed Qing, not believing her sister was having such a hard time. The Archer noticed Hung's controlling way over her and separated the two. He took Qing off to a corner of the field, and they spoke for a while until her eyes easily looked upon him as their conversation continued. Soon, she returned to the target area. Qing lifted her bow with a sense of confidence. Hung had noticed her sister was calm and focused, and there were no more rubber-band faces. This time, as she let the string go, her arrow hit the target dead-on.

Rushing to Qing, Hung asked, "What did he say to change you in only minutes?"

Qing just looked at her, giving a sheepish smile and continued shooting with success. The Archer smiled to see the two of them interact and was pleased that Qing had heard his every word. Eventually, Qing shared her secret with her sister, telling her of the Archer's words. "It is all in your mind," she said. "Think of what you want to happen, and believe in yourself. Your mind controls everything you do. Make your thoughts into whatever you want, and remember intent is everything."

Armin turned his mind to thoughts of Zu-Ling, who had taken the first steps in learning to forgive himself and to understand that his controlled mind would allow him all that he desired. Within the purity of his thoughts, he could manifest all things. The Archer knew the young man desired to be like the many men he had known from a distance in his years of growing. Unfortunately, he never had anyone to guide him along his path. Zu-Ling was intrigued by this European stranger with graying blond hair, who knew nothing of him, yet easily chose to guide him as a father would guide his own son. Finding comfort and caring from the Archer, Zu-Ling felt honored. He learned patience with himself, while understanding that all people were the same and there was no difference between them. This first day, he learned to listen, not resist, realizing that we were all there to help one another, not to fight each other.

The Archer felt gratitude as he looked through the small window at his bedside and watched the glistening stars dance upon the velvet sky. Soon, his heavy eyes and weary body drifted into another dimension. This night was filled with dreams that disrupted the Archer's sleep. He tossed and turned, as perspiration covered his body. Sitting upright in his bed, he took a deep breath, as he tried to pull himself back into reality. His heart pounded, and his body tingled as chills rippled through him. Thunder rumbled in the distance, although the sky was clear. He listened intently to its rhythm and all the sounds of the night.

The window next to him was small and offered a view of a burning light from a room that extended from the main house. As he was watching the light flicker and fade, a silhouette appeared at the window. The Archer watched Lihua brushing her long hair as she readied for bed. Slowly, she began to remove her silk robe, gently sliding it from her shoulders. Trapped in the scene, he was unable to move his eyes from her. Hai then appeared from behind; leaning down, he turned her head from side to side, kissing her cheeks softly. His lips followed the contour of her slender neck, as he turned her toward him. Their lips melted into one. Taking Lihua's hand, Hai escorted her out of sight. The scene had taken its place with the Archer, and his breathing deepened as he tried to calm his rapidly beating heart. Lying there, he sensed an overwhelming loneliness, remembering a time when love had filled him. These thoughts belonged to the past, and his wish was to let them go back to a locked box somewhere deep within his heart. Quickly turning his attention away from the sensitive scene, Armin gazed out at the moonlit sky where stars brightly arranged themselves, making pictures on the vast velvet palette of the universe. Thunder rumbled in the distance, mesmerizing him as he slumped down into a supine position, finding peace in the sleep that overcame him.

Dawn, as always, came quickly, and Armin lay listening to the beginning of a new day, not wanting to move.

Nearby, songbirds filled the cool air with their melodies and the splashing sounds of a waterfall hitting upon the rocks as the river pushed its way downstream. These were the very same sounds that had filled his head in Bavaria so long ago, the ones he had heard when he sat in the forest at his secret pond. Listening, he was washed with the exact sensations that had stirred his soul when he stood on the bridge overlooking the Danube River. The Archer felt comforted by these thoughts, yet sadness tugged at him. He knew his time in China would soon come to an end. He chose to put such thoughts out of his head, knowing God would guide what was to be in the right time. He then arose, stretching his body and feeling every muscle pulling and tugging, some with great discomfort. He surmised it was simply the bed that was stiff and old, which led him to feel the same. He would not complain of this but work out the kinks himself.

From the workshop, he stepped outside the narrow doorway. Feeling the early morning light upon him, he took his place with nature. Beginning the slow movements of Taijiquan, he relaxed while releasing his sore muscles. His body flowed like a gentle river moving onward into obscurity, as one motion moved into the next, having no beginning and no end. The music he heard was made by the sounds of buzzing bees, singing birds, and the alarmed cawing of a crow in the early morning hours. Rustling leaves swirled like a cyclone around his feet, adding to the ensemble of sounds. Closing his eyes, Armin took all of nature into him, welcoming his new day.

Suddenly, he felt eyes upon him, interrupting his concentration. Turning slowly, he met the eyes of Meifeng and Bolin, who were in a serious state as they mimicked his every move. The Archer realized they too often practiced this martial art form for they were familiar with each of the moves calling them by their proper names. Taijiquan was a tool used for grounding and flowing as one with the universe. After several more moves, a wave of gentle giggles quickly turned into belly laughs as their tiny hands covered their mouths. The Archer too could not resist the moment and found himself smiling as he nodded to the children.

A cough and throat clearing ended the moment. They turned, looking behind themselves to see a stern gaze turn into a beaming smile that glowed across Lihua's face. Her hands and eyes then motioned them inside. For a moment, the Archer stared at Lihua's face, remembering the window scene from the night before. He found himself blushing as he pulled his eyes from her. She in turn gazed briefly and then looked down at the earth. Again, she was drawn to look at his face and into the depth of his blue eyes, which fascinated her. It was then that she knew beyond all doubt that he shared in knowing the intimacy she lived.

Sunday morning, the table was filled with many foods of brilliant colors, and the aromas of mixed herbs and sweetbreads filled the entire house. Hai looked toward the Archer, bowing his head, as all closed their eyes in a moment of thanksgiving. Without conversation, each began to take their fill of food and drink. Only eyes and the tilt of a head would ask another to pass a platter from the far side of the table. Soon, breakfast ended, and the children were anxious to return to the field. Lihua motioned for them to help clean off the table.

The Archer and Hai remained sitting. They were engaged in a conversation regarding the positive changes they had both seen in Zu-Ling. Hai explained that Zu-ling's father had died when he was very young. His mother worked long hours each day at a factory far from their home. Zu-Ling had been raised by his aged grandmother, who spoiled him terribly. She was tired and struggled to fulfill the arduous job of parenting. She felt sad for him knowing he needed the direction and guidance of two loving parents. For this, his grandmother would often cry, wishing time and better health were on her side. During the day, Zu-Ling confided only a small part of his story, permitting the Archer to write the rest in his mind. The Archer was not concerned about Zu-Ling's past, although he had empathy for the difficulties in his life. He was interested only in the direction the young man was headed. The Archer knew the changes Zu-Ling would need to make and the lessons he needed to learn if he were to become a man of honor. This would mean putting aside his ego and finding the true warrior within himself. He looked at the children who were busy helping Lihua and asked them to come to the table so that he could share his thoughts with them. "Remember," he said, "make your decisions wisely, for each passing moment of time is gone forever, and you will never be able to undo what has been done."

They all stopped what they were doing. Looking at one another, they wondered who this man, who was followed by Silverhawk and gifted with so much wisdom, truly was. Lihua then broke the silence as she began taking more bowls and utensils from the table. Soon, all were in motion and moving again toward the open field to learn more of the Archer's way. Upon his arrival, the Archer looked happily at the smiling faces of the children and their parents, all of whom waited for more instructions. One by one, they lined up as he began to teach. "This bow is a part of you. Holding it permits you to take on the spirit of the wood. Honor it, as you are one. Intend your arrow to make its mark, and then release the thought. You will see that your arrow will find its way." Zu-Ling was listening; he was confused, wondering how this could be. The Archer approached him, and they walked far away from the crowd in deep conversation while the others began to practice. Soon, the expression on Zu-Ling's face showed an easiness and understanding between the two.

Rejoining Hai's relatives, the Archer noticed Meifeng standing and watching everyone; she had no bow. The Archer then turned to one of Meifeng's cousins and asked to borrow his bow, then extending his hand he invited her to shoot. At first, she refused, only to give in to his offer. She took the bow now without hesitation; it was as if she already had a relationship with it. All eyes were upon her as she stepped forward. Meifeng eyed the target beyond and then raised the bow, pulling back the string with perfection until her finger met the corner of her lip. She then released her arrow, which easily found its mark. The others raised their voices, praising the young girl's accomplishment. Zu-Ling looked at her in amazement, never expecting such success and asked how she could do this without any true practice. She answered, "I listened to the Archer, to my intention, and to my heart. It is fun, and I don't take it too seriously, as you do. Zu-Ling," she said, "open your mind and your heart. Have you not heard the words of the teacher?"

Lihua and Hai looked at each other, happy to hear this explanation from Meifeng, understanding she was growing into a woman of knowledge and wisdom.

Walking toward Bolin, she smiled at her parents, knowing they were pleased with her. Extending her arm, she offered Bolin the bow, giving him a chance to prove his skills. Bolin took the bow and began moving his hands over the wood as the Archer had taught them. His eyes were bright and gleaming at the opportunity. A serious look overtook him, and his concentration locked onto the target beyond. Pulling back the string, his arms began to shake and wobble. The Archer immediately knew the draw weight of the bow was too much for Bolin and exchanged it for one of lesser weight. Finding his proper posture and synchronized breathing, Bolin pulled the string with ease. His arrow flew and hit the target just off to the left of the bull's-eye. Bolin looked at his teacher, who gave a nod of approval. The Archer turned toward Hai and Lihua and handed each a bow. Hai was already an archer with experience and knowledge of shooting. Along with the others, he too learned from the Archer more about breathing and the part it played in making the shot. In addition, Hai now understood how to root himself and empty his mind, something he had never been able to do completely before. Lihua, however, was shy and reserved in taking the bow. She was not athletically inclined but was willing to learn. The Archer showed patience with her, guiding each segment of the shot. Soon, she took aim and was successful, feeling a great sense of accomplishment. Smiling, she thanked the Archer for his kindness. Lihua's eyes fell to the ground; without looking up at her teacher, she simply held her hand out, giving the bow back to him. Whispering, she said, "I am finished with my experience."

On the small hill above the target area, Zu-Ling and Meifeng found themselves shooting against one another in a match of skills. They seemed to laugh a lot and have success with their arrows, which pleased the Archer. He concluded that it took a young woman to enlighten Zu-Ling's spirit, allowing him to see what was always before him. As the sun began falling behind the tall pines, they all returned to their homes before nightfall.

The Archer reflected on the day and was satisfied that Zu-Ling was now more accepted by the others. During his days of learning, he began to show humility and patience. He had also found a new friend in Meifeng. The Archer then allowed his thoughts to fade as he focused on the certainty that a wonderful dinner awaited, and as he suspected, Lihua had made a delicious meal for her family and guest.

Photo by Armin Hirmer

After dinner, they sat for a short while conversing as Lihua prepared tea and sweets for the table. Insisting on helping in some small way, the Archer asked if he could prepare a formal tea ceremony. Surprised, Lihua nodded and took a rosewood tea tray from the shelf of the cabinet. The Archer began preparing for the tea ceremony by placing the cups and the teapots Lihua had gathered. From the counter, she took jars of different varieties of loose-leaf tea. Placing each in its own container, she gave them to her guest. He arranged five tea cups in the front part of the tray and then placed one teapot to the right side and another to the left. Lihua brought heated water to the table. Its temperature was perfect for brewing. Slowly, the Archer poured the water into each bowl, one by one, cleaning the clay. Then carefully, he dropped tea leaves in the bottom of the pot and brewed them for only a few seconds. He strained the tea leaves carefully as he poured the tea and offered each person a cup. Watching in surprise, they concluded that the Archer was an expert with the techniques of brewing and cleaning each cup and pot, upholding Chinese tradition.

Evening had once again come to an end. The Archer retired to the comfort of his sleeping place. He was happy for the success of Hai's family and confident that his work there was complete. Outside his small window, he looked to the sky and to Big Bear, his favorite constellation. He sent his heart's desire and inner most secrets far out into the universe as he spoke to the night sky. After closing his eyes, he slept for only a short time without any dreams to disturb him. Morning came with the softness of singing birds, and he enjoyed the sound of their waking hymns. Arising early, he knew his departure from Hai's home was to be within moments. Somehow, he felt compelled to move on toward a new place, one which he would call home for a short time. Not knowing where he was going, he followed the path Silverhawk set for him. A plan lay waiting; it was not of his hand but of God's choosing. There would be a new place, one where he was needed and where his gifts would be useful. Slowly, he gathered his things, making certain all his belongings were packed tightly in his satchel. With one more glance, he looked around the room that had brought him comfort and warmth and felt gratitude for the kind hospitality shown him. Quietly, the Archer slipped off into the forest on an unknown pathway. His eyes searched the morning sky to find Silverhawk circling above. Good-byes did not have a place with the Archer, and never would he permit emotion of any kind to overtake him. Instead, he focused on the newness of the hope and promise that lay ahead, where he would give something of himself back to the world, kindling the human spirit with his teachings of the bow.

# Chapter Seven

## A Pathway Home

*T*he Archer felt indebted to the people of Wudang, its mountains, and the monks. In his parting, he left behind pieces of his heart and his spirit. During his walk off the mountain, he heard the shrilling cries of Silverhawk. Looking skyward, the Archer found the great bird flying overhead and followed the path marked by the birds' flight. He trusted the guidance given, assuring him safe passage toward civilization. Many times, the trail's thick foliage did not leave a clear path for the Archer to follow, so he watched the position of the sun and listened for the rush of a nearby river. As he hiked into the depth of the forest, he saw deer and other wildlife foraging for their daily morsels. Foxes and coyotes were everywhere, but never did he raise his bow against them. These hunters in turn only looked his way briefly as they continued on in search of food.

As the Archer made his way out of the forest, Meifeng and Bolin went to the room where their guest had slept. They knocked on the door gently, but there was no answer. Slowly, they lifted the latch, opening the door quietly, just enough to poke their heads inside, finding it empty of his belongings. The blanket made by Lihua was folded at the end of the bed as it had been the first day. The sweet grass pillow case lay at the head of the bed, flat, and its contents missing. At the center of the bed lay one single lotus blossom which brought a hint of life to the room. The Archer was gone! Panicked, the children ran as fast as they could out the small doorway of the workshop, thinking surely he must be there doing his morning ritual of Taijiquan. They found only the mound of sweet grass that had filled his pillow lying scattered on the ground. Running to the kitchen, they were certain he would be eating breakfast. His place at the table was vacant. With only one last place to look, they ran like the wind to the field beyond the house hoping to find him shooting his bow and arrows. The scene before them was empty now, and so were their hearts. Tears flowed from both as they looked upon the one target left on the field. Bolin ran to it, seeing something glistening in the newness of the sun's rays. A golden arrow sat in the bull's-eye. Pulling the arrow from its resting place, he studied it. There in the corner just under the feathers was an inscription. Bolin, even at his young age, knew the meaning of the message left behind. Grabbing the arrow tightly, he held it close to his chest; briefly, he wondered if Meifeng would argue to whom it would belong. She looked at her brother, smiling as she held up the lotus blossom then gently placed it in her hair. Bolin understood her gesture and was happy with his gift. Meifeng pointed to a long, thin package wrapped in a brown bag, which rested on the top of the target. She took it from its perch and found Zu-Ling's name in large print near the closure. Holding the package tightly, she took it with her as she and her brother ran to tell their parents the news of the Archer's disappearance.

Hai and Lihua shared in their sadness when told of their guest's departure, but they explained that this archer had a world of places to visit. "He is the Bow Whisperer, the teacher of many," Hai said. "We cannot be selfish in keeping him here with us. Behind, he has left all of us with knowledge of new ways with the bow. He has also mended one young man's spirit. The Archer will always remain with us, as he has changed many things in his short stay. Those things will be with us forever. A small part of him will never leave." The children were comforted by this thought and promised to hold close the memory of the one who had laughed at their antics and taught them not only how to use the bow with respect but also how to find their own spirit.

Deep in the forest, Armin had already traveled for five hours following the path Silverhawk had marked for him. Eventually, human voices echoed in the near distance. He found himself climbing up a small hill as branches and low brush grabbed at his clothing, as though not wanting him to leave. Pulling his pant legs from the clutches of barbed brush and gnarled vines, he freed himself. Stretched out before him was a long, dusty road just wide enough for the passage of two horse-drawn carts or perhaps two small modern vehicles. Armin's instincts led him to take a left upon leaving the dense forest walking toward the heart of town. Along his way, he occasionally met others busy with their daily chores. Some meandered with goats or sheep on their way to a grazing pasture or to market. Wondering if they had seen a ghost, they stared at the foreigner, not knowing who he was. His white skin and blond-streaked hair were enough to startle them, but when he looked into their eyes with a greeting of kindness, their jaws fell. Blue eyes had almost never been seen in this part of the world. He simply smiled and then nodded, continuing on his way as they stood like statues in the middle of the road watching his even, tireless stride from behind. Armin watched Silverhawk circle above him and soar into the distance, guiding him to his final destination.

Ahead, he heard the noise of the city clamoring in his ears. He dreaded large crowds and noisy confusion, preferring the quiet of the forest or the serenity he felt as he watched the rhythm of an ocean wave. Soon, he became lost in the crowd of thousands, feeling the city had swallowed him whole.

Armin's time in Wudang had come to its end. Lost in thought, his hands fumbled with the papers he held as he waited in a long line of passengers preparing to board the aircraft. Heavyhearted, he wondered if there was another place on earth offering the same beauty and peace he had found in China. Sitting high off the tarmac, he remained deep in thought as he gazed from the aircraft's window. Armin was burrowed in a large gray leather seat awaiting takeoff. The sun glistened on the silver wings of the plane, blinding his sight momentarily. Yes, he acknowledged his sadness at leaving this country rich in history and tradition from times of an ancient past. The philosophy of the Tao and the ideals of the mountain people had profoundly changed him. Feeling centered, Armin realized more than ever that simplicity and love were more than enough to fill him. His life in Germany had been successful, and he felt gratitude for his past. However, that part of his life was behind him now. He focused on his experiences and the knowledge he had gained of the martial arts during his stay in China, knowing the many lessons would be bound with the wisdom of his soul. Armin felt passionate about giving back to humanity whatever he could. His compassion for those less fortunate weighed on his heart. Never would he look for recognition or praise; he desired only to make a small difference in the life of another. Armin felt that to bring a smile or laugher to someone's heart for even the briefest of moments was a step toward love.

The flight attendant passed down the aisle, checking the passengers, making certain all seat backs were up and seat belts fastened. She spoke to Armin softly; yet he did not hear her. She lightly tapped him on the shoulder, and he turned to acknowledge her. His eyes were moist with tears. Righting his seat back, he buckled himself in safely. Then without words, he resumed staring out the window, gazing toward the mountains in the distance. Soon, the engines roared and the plane began to taxi down the bumpy runway. Full throttle, the plane gently lifted into the sky, ending Armin's experience in a land of great richness and wonder.

## Chapter Eight

# Regensburg

For most, home would be a place of comfort and peace, yet for Armin, his return to Regensburg was bittersweet. At times, reflection overtook him when remembering the negativity that had devoured him in what now seemed to be a lifetime ago. It was never his way to think back on the past, but on this day, he embraced his feelings on the subject of home, trying to rationalize a deep-rooted gnawing in the pit of his stomach. The discomfort he felt would only settle with meditation along with readjustments of his thoughts. He knew that one could never change the past; Armin's only desire was to heal all negative memories from his earlier years, allowing them to sleep forever. Once he reached into the depths of himself, he felt different being on the soil of his homeland. A peaceful settling had come upon him, and with the passing of time, Armin had matured by returning to the roots of his youth. He experienced a rebirth from the times he was lost to a commercial world. Ten years of learned studies guided by martial arts and his change from Catholicism to the philosophy of the Tao Te Ching opened a new world of understanding for him. His life had been changed forever.

Happy times and modest contentment now filled Armin's new life in Regensburg. His many friends had gathered, giving him a warm welcome home, for which he was grateful. As always, his days began with Taijiquan and the quiet gathering of chi, which opened him to receive wisdom from the universe. Aware that all things in life were connected with the flow of yin and yang energies, Armin often imagined intertwining his way of the bow and his spiritual beliefs with all of life. He wrote manuals and used his drawings to depict each thought, bringing life's circle to a perfect completion.

Nighttime found Armin empty-minded, drifting away from all consciousness. Within the void of nothingness, voices and images from Wudang came calling, beckoning for his return. The spirit of the mountains was powerful and enlightening, which gave him total peace. As he recalled the simple life of solitude and natural comfort, he yearned to return to that mystical place. Armin remembered the vow he had made to himself as he hiked many miles from the home of Hai and Lihua. And again, he promised to find a way to give back to the great country of China. The high mountains of Wudang had given Armin a new strength and knowledge as he learned the truth of the warrior who lived within him.

In time, Armin blended back into the pace of Regensburg, working once again, but this time, far from his old career in architecture. He was a teacher and master of the bow, of Taijiquan, and of the tea ceremony, all of which he offered to his students. Each day was a classroom of opportunity to learn more of life's mysteries. By meshing his past and present knowledge, he found great success with his new business. Using the proceeds from his teachings to help the less fortunate in Wudang, he fulfilled his promise by setting up a foundation.

On weekends, Armin renewed himself by walking city streets, making certain to enjoy the magnificent architecture so rich in Germany. He appreciated the intricacy of fine art and thought of the great artists who made their mark by leaving their treasures for all to enjoy. Eventually, he found himself standing on the bridge over the Danube River, watching the sunset and listening to the waters below him. There, he reveled in wonder and gratitude for all that was. Armin looked to the skies to find Silverhawk soaring above, calling out with piercing sounds a welcoming. The two had been apart for months, but this day, they were again as one.

**His Path**

Three years had found their way behind him. Armin's teachings in Germany began replicating themselves, becoming mundane and stifling for him. His spirit of adventure and desire for novelty in his life were on the rise once again. He yearned for change, understanding he was needed elsewhere in the world. There was a stirring at his very core, an intuition. In his quiet moments of deep reflection, an echoing from the universe filled his soul, affirming that he needed to take heed. As usual, Armin would have a thought one day, pack up, and move the next, as this was his way. Saying nothing, he gathered his belongings, few though they were, and began traveling the Romantic Road, which wound its way through cities and small villages in Bavaria. During his many days of travel to the south, he enjoyed the scenery and the people he met along his way.

Armin headed to Lech, Austria, which bordered his native Germany. A friend of his who owned a sports club there had asked Armin if he would come to teach his staff the philosophy of intent in the proper techniques of shooting. He would easily share the wisdom of the Tao Te Ching and of martial arts, which was a part of his life, woven as one with the bow.

Lech, a beautiful village, graced by majestic snowcapped mountains, whose peaks hid themselves in clouds as they reached to touch the blue sky, was a paradise for skiers. Snow fell in the middle of August. Armin loved to walk, and wherever he went, he took on the roadways and sidewalks of cities, villages, seaports, and mountains, pounding his feet to the ground as he celebrated all of life. Each scene his eyes captured was a gift to be treasured. Time off from the sports club took him to the peaks above Lech where deer dotted the mountain ranges. The famous British sculptor Anthony Gormley made metal statues of naked men in his own likeness. One hundred of these statues speckled the ranges in the higher altitudes. As Armin looked at them in wonder, he grinned and simply moved along, never judging the way of another. In his travels, he met welcoming families. They were fascinated by this humble man who enjoyed fresh air and long walks through pastures and mountain passes. In his wake, he always left a smile and kind word behind.

Exploring the ancient village on his return from the mountains, Armin stopped for his morning mocha with a breakfast of scones and blackberry jam. He took pleasure in watching people come and go, being entertained by their amusing antics and interactions with one another. Soon, the crowds began to gather on an open green across from the Cathedral of St. Nicholas's. A large, colorful banner announced a fundraiser for the less fortunate in the city. It briefly described activities for young and old alike. In the distance, he heard music playing as the gaiety of life filled the atmosphere.

After finishing his breakfast, Armin returned to the sports club to gather his things and say farewell to his friends. He then left the city as he had come into it, carrying only a small black bag and a long sleeve, which protected his bows and arrows. On his way out of town, he came upon the festivities at St. Nicholas's. He had arrived in time to see the delight on the children's faces as they watched magicians and jugglers work their magic. The children created quite a scene of hysteria and laughter, twisting and contorting themselves to the amusement of the performers and bringing a smile to Armin's face. Armin sat for a time on a grassy hill gazing out into the crowds of people below. Within a short time, he was no longer alone.

Just as the geese had done at the forest pond long ago, the children began to gather one by one to sit by his side. They wondered who this stranger was and waited for him to speak to them. Armin said a simple "Hello" and began taking his bows from their sleeve. The hill area was open and safe for shooting; a loosely wrapped bale of hay would suffice as a target. The children were excited and begged for a chance to shoot the arrows. Armin did not disappoint them, teaching each in turn. Amazed at how quickly they learned, the children felt a sense of pride at having placed their arrows on the target.

Suddenly, horrifying screams pierced the peacefulness of the day, easily reaching the hillside set high above the crowds. A scuffle broke out nearby, and a teen lay bleeding from a head wound on the path below. Andrew Wiles, a young boy of simple mind with deformed legs was often the target of bullies. His mother hovered over him screaming and praying for him to move, to get up. Her sobs echoed as everyone ran to assist the fallen child. Some only looked with pity while others brought cool water to rouse the young lad. A doctor in the crowd came to lend his expertise, taking Andrew's pulse and listening for a heartbeat. But stillness prevailed.

Armin stood up from his perch on the hillside and walked down to the pathway below, making his way to the young boy. The crowd parted, widening a path for the stranger. Armin looked upon the boy, who lay lifeless. Taking a wet cloth offered by another, he bent down next to

Andrew and wiped his brow. Moving closer, Armin placed his mouth near the boy's ear and whispered something no one else could hear. In moments, the young boy began to move his legs. The doctor, who had moved out of the way to make room for the stranger, looked upon him in disbelief and asked, "What did you say to bring such a spontaneous reaction?" Moments later, screams of joy came from the child's anguished mother. Andrew's eyes flinched and then fluttered open. Fear shot through him, and he began to flail his arms. The boy made grunting noises, not understood by anyone. A quiet then came upon him as he tried to get up. Stretching out his arms, he turned his head from side to side, looking for the one who had whispered to him. Without warning, he called for his mother, who immediately cradled her crippled son in her arms, as onlookers sighed with relief. All turned in wonder at this stranger, hoping to thank him for his help, but he was gone. Armin was lost in the multitudes, following the flight of Silverhawk as he flew above the crowd of people; in moments, the bird circled in one place.

At the place Silverhawk marked from the sky, Armin found a group of young men laughing loudly and telling jokes for all to hear. As Armin approached, he noticed one tall, handsome boy boasting to the others that he had taken the cripple down. The young man was holding his bloody hands as though they were a prize given for the cruelty he had shown Andrew Wiles. Armin asked him how he injured himself. The boy became irritated that anyone, especially a stranger, would have the nerve to ask him this or any other question. Defensively, his friends clustered around as if a fight would break out. Each watched the blond stranger, with the eyes of wolves. Armin simply asked, "Is this your way?"

The boy looked at him and said, "This is none of your business. What do you mean my 'way'? Why, stranger, do you speak to me in riddles?"

Armin continued, "I mean, you have chosen cruelty over kindness. You have chosen to boast of your deed. Another lies injured at your hand, and you have no compassion or regret for your actions. What is it in your own life that has made you become so uncaring and thoughtless toward others?"

"Fredric!" the others taunted. "Teach this man a lesson! Take him down!" they hollered.

The group circled Armin, and from behind, one attacked forcefully. One, with the eyes of a wolf, found himself flat out on the ground. The others were shocked at Armin's speed. Baffled, they wondered how he could react so fast, as he had no way of seeing the attacker coming. The others took on this challenge, certain they could defeat the stranger, but each in his own turn stared at the brown earth, gasping for a breath of air and groaning in pain. Armin stood above them as a group of teenage girls looked on, giggling at the sight of the boys lying on the floor of Mother Earth, rolling about.

"You have reaped what you have sown," Armin said in the calm yet reprimanding voice of a father. "What was the purpose of this? Now you too are humiliated, embarrassed, and must recover from the pain you suffer. Now you feel like the lame boy. Hurt not only bodily, but also you are without pride and being laughed at and mocked by others. Your ego crushed. How does this feel?" Armin asked. "It would be wise to look back and seek the answers you need. Know the reason why you have chosen this path. Is it that another has injured you in the same way and you know no different than to behave so poorly? Think!" Armin demanded. "And realize your own truth."

Accompanied by the flight of Silverhawk, Armin walked away, losing himself in the crowd as he headed back to his perch on the hillside. The children had waited for his return, guarding his bow and arrows. Upon his arrival, they asked for more knowledge and another chance to practice. Happily, he agreed.

Fredric eventually was able to sit upright. Ashamed, he moved, hiding from the others and taking refuge beneath a large oak tree. He stayed there for some time thinking as Armin had insisted. His eyes welled with tears that spilled over and streamed down his cheeks. In his silence, he thought back to the misery of his home life. His own father had mistreated him horribly since he was very young and still would lay a heavy hand on him. Fredric tried to make sense of the reason his father had no control over himself. He twisted his mind trying to find the answers as to why his father would lash out at him. He had been tormented mentally and physically; scars and bruises marred his battered body. The young rebel felt shame, knowing his father drank too much, and in this, he became a different person, someone Fredric no longer recognized. He knew full well that his mother took the brunt of her husband's wrath, especially when she tried to protect her children. Fredric was the youngest, and she did her best to protect him from his father's drunken rage. With each intervention, her husband's fury became more intense. As time went on, she withdrew and lived her life as if her feet were bound with cloth, her life snuffed out. Fredric's mother, Marian, wore the same scars and bruises as her son. She was a broken woman, far too frail to fight for her right to live with dignity. Being unable to give love and support to her beloved children or to protect them from her husband nearly destroyed her. Marian's pain was that of a broken heart, and there could be no growth for her, only a life of subtle slavery and dysfunction for the entire family. She succumbed to a place that bred unhappiness and discontent, anguished by both physical and mental abuse, which pushed her life force from her. Fredric had lost the laughter of his mother, her encouraging and loving ways. Both were bound to one another yet cheated of their ability to show love and the unity of family. His father, who fought his own internal demons, simply would not permit expressions of love and caring, wanting each to be as miserable as he was. Fredric and Marian longed for a life without conflict or the obstacles that had been thrown their way.

Soon, the movie in Fredric's mind slowed and faded away. Leaving the lofty shade of the oak tree, he ambled among the swarms of people to look for Andrew Wiles.

As he walked, his eyes stared at the path of grass and dirt beneath his feet. Fredric realized then that he had taken his frustrations and anger out on an innocent victim and that he too was a victim of his own father's hand. Shame filled him as he thought about the pain he had inflicted on the younger boy. Fredric needed to right his actions. At last, his eyes fell upon Andrew. He was sitting with a small group of people who continued to ask about the incident. Some stood as Fredric approached; looks of fear crossed their otherwise startled faces. The group of boys moved away, leaving Andrew alone to face his attacker, but not too far in case he might need them. Andrew sat looking up at his assailant, suspecting he would apologize but put his hand up stopping him from doing so. Instead, in a calm, yet strong voice, he said, "I forgive you."

Fredric was dumbfounded, never expecting to hear these words. "How can it be? I was cruel and humiliated you. Look! You are injured!"

Andrew smiled and said, "You humiliated yourself, Fredric."

Again, Fredric flinched in disbelief as he tried to explain. "I have come to apologize for my actions. I was wrong, and I am so sorry." Hearing this, Andrew's mother came near to stand by her son. Fredric tearfully told Mrs. Wiles that he envied the attention she gave her son and that he missed the love of his own mother and the attention she had once so freely given him.

Mrs. Wiles was saddened; her lips began to tremble, and tears gently streamed down her face. She took Fredric's hand in her own. A warm smile met his face as she thanked him for the sincerity of his apology. She placed his hand into Andrew's saying, "Go, and enjoy the rest of the day. It will do you both good."

Together, Andrew and Fredric went up the hill to find the stranger. On their way, Fredric asked Andrew, "How could you so easily forgive what I have done to you?"

Andrew smiled saying, "I heard a voice when lying on the ground and it said, and 'To be free is to forgive, so forgive him.' What else could it have meant if not to forgive you, Fredric?"

There, upon the hill, they found the stranger teaching the children who had gathered to shoot the bow. They all listened intently to the words the Archer spoke. Armin looked up as the boys approached. Nodding his head in approval, he handed each a bow and set of arrows saying, "Now you will learn to empty your mind of all things, becoming one with yourself and with the universe. It is *intent* that matters." Armin taught more than just how to hold a bow and place an arrow on the string. He taught about wisdom and patience using valuable tools for calming oneself. He instructed them on how to feel and be in the present moment, not only for the sport of archery but in their everyday lives as well. He stressed kindness and taught about sharing. Armin discouraged arguments, encouraging them to find a peaceful way to resolve their problems. Often, he spoke of the ancient Chinese and their customs, telling how each bow comes alive in the hands of an archer. "It is said that a bow takes on the spirit of the one who holds it, bringing it new life and energy." Armin loved to watch the faces of the children as he told his stories of archery. The children were in awe of his tales. They had seen such things on television and at the movies, but being able to shoot made their fantasies a reality, giving each a sense of accomplishment.

Time flew, and the sun began to sink in the sky, ending another day. The children begged for Armin to return the next day so they might learn and practice more of his way with the bow. With pleading eyes, Fredric and Andrew also longed for his return. As the children went on their way, Armin stood alone on the hillside, watching until each had disappeared out of sight. Night was soon approaching, so Armin gathered up his sparse belongings from the hillside, packing his bows and arrows. He then disappeared into the twilight of the day. Confident that nature would blanket him in protection, he merged with the forest. Once again, he was being called to move on. Guided by his soul, he knew best where he would be useful. Armin never questioned the guidance he received but would go on alone to serve as he could.

> "I am here to serve, I am here to inspire. I am here to love. I am here to live my truth."
>
> —Deepak Chopra

The next day of celebration brought music and an atmosphere of happiness to the church of St. Nicholas. Fredric and Andrew found one another in the crowd and began to walk toward the hill where Armin had taught the day before. Patiently, Fredric waited for Andrew, who was faltering with his cane. He still had pain from the injuries he sustained the previous day. Fredric offered his arm to Andrew. No words were needed as Andrew's eyes brightly gleamed in appreciation. Guilt suddenly came upon Fredric like a wave from the ocean that might catch one from behind. Quickly, he remembered the words of the Archer, "Forgive yourself for having acted in such a cruel way." Fredric promised in silence to change his ways forever.

Reaching the top of the hill, they found the other children had gathered and were waiting for the Archer's return. Some occupied themselves by playing soccer while Fredric scanned the hilltop looking out into the crowds below. Still, there was no sign of the Archer anywhere. Looking toward the far end of the field, Fredric spotted something glistening from the hay target. Andrew followed, trying to catch up with his friends' long strides. A golden arrow with words carved on its shaft beamed out at him. Fredric knew the meaning behind the message and realized it was for him. "Be not like any other man; forgive yourself." Looking at Andrew, Fredric offered the arrow to him.

Andrew put his hand up and said, "I have his words here," tapping his heart. "You take his arrow." And so it was.

Armin had rested in the comfort of the forest the previous night, hoping his message was heard and understood by both boys. As always, sadness overcame him each time he moved on, but he was confident these young men would find their way. His work had been completed in the village of Lech. He would again follow the path Silverhawk laid for him.

# Chapter Nine

# Moving On

*A*rmin's dreams were many during his night in the forest, leaving him tired before the start of his new journey. Nearly unable to gather enough chi to continue traveling without difficulty, he ate berries from a nearby bush and drank water from a mountain stream. Sitting for a moment, he was certain he had heard the voice of the Great One during his long, restless night, a voice guiding him toward the sea. Armin silently agreed, knowing the tropical weather would be more agreeable to his bones. He preferred warm, balmy breezes found only on ocean shores. Such a wonderful thought brought visions of rolling waves and long stretches of beach for him to walk. Each day's end would be a great gift; he would watch as the sun set over the water, sinking into the horizon, giving him a sense of completeness and becoming one with all that is. There were times along Armin's path when his heart would find happiness with those he met along his way. He wished he could stay longer merely to extend the friendships he had made. Somehow, he knew his course and what God had intended for him.

Armin awoke to the singing of birds and the smells of fresh pine needles, which he had piled high to make a soft bed for his comfort. Upon standing, he slowly began moving his body in fluid patterns with no beginnings and no endings. Taijiquan gave him vital energy, filling him each day for all that lay ahead. Armin walked many long hours during the day, which was exhausting. He would rest only if the scene suited him. Finding a rocky ledge that overlooked flowered fields that swayed in rhythm to the stirring of the breeze, he stretched his weary body. Reaching his face toward the sun, he breathed new life into every pore of his body, relishing the life that so freely swirled around him. Peacefulness soaked through to his soul, and gratitude hugged him. At times like these—and there were many— he would stand, take up his bow, and send an arrow out to the universe where it flew freely through the air, releasing his spirit to the entire world.

Armin Hirmer

## Journey to the Sea

Armin walked for many miles and occasionally hitchhiked along the narrow roads that wound through villages and towns along his way. A stranger had offered him a ride in his rickety old truck, for which Armin was grateful. He was glad to be sitting in comfort and resting his sore feet. Regretfully, the driver's journey ended long before they reached Armin's final destination. He was appreciative of the stranger's kindness, and they shook hands as each went his separate way. Armin stood alone in the road, watching the old blue truck continue on its journey, knowing he would spend at least one more lonely night on a grassy bed on the forest floor before he reached his destination.

One more night beneath the stars was all he could tolerate, so he made the best of his situation and found the perfect place. This time, he chose an open field bordered by tall pines. He made his pillow of soft fir boughs and gathered long reeds of grass, which he stuffed into the sleeves of his jacket. Once settled, Armin lay looking at the sky as he created pictures made of stars to bring him comfort. Cascades of meteors streaked through the velvet night, assisting time's passage to a quickened dawn. Sleep eventually found its way to him, and dreams filled his head once more. His ear pressed to the earth, he began to hear the thunder of hundreds of horse hooves pounding their way toward him. Roaring voices screamed in a language only vaguely familiar to him, metal swords clanked as they hit one another, and the anguished cries of men in battle echoed filling the stale air. Fear ricocheted through him as he thrashed his body upright; grabbing at his throat, he screamed, yet there was no sound to be heard. Finally, he bellowed, breaking the silence of the night as sweat dripped from his naked chest. Deliriously, Armin tried to still the abnormal beating of his heart as he attempted to find his way back to reality. Soon, the cooing of a night owl soothed him, permitting him the rest he so desperately needed. Was this creature of the night perched above real or a spirit guide? They continued to watch one another until finally Armin's eyes fell closed, bringing him to a place beyond this earth.

Taken by Mdf http://en.wikipedia.org/wiki/File:Strix-varia-005.jpg

## Chapter Ten

# First Encounter

*U*pon the dawning of the next day, the Archer was determined to know the meaning of the dreams that had brought him such unrest. These dreams had haunted him for years. Since his visit to Wudang, they had become more and more frequent, leaving him to feel an intimacy with them.

Ambling along the path leading to civilization, the Archer was led to a glacial lake that mirrored the images of the snowcapped Alps. He sat and watched the waters, allowing himself time to drift in an awakened state of awareness. There, within the confines of his mind, images came to him. They were of men wearing colorful robes of silk, which fell elegantly to the floor. Some were dressed in long, baggy pants with mandarin-collared shirts. The men had long black hair pulled back into a braid away from their faces. To the right were walls of rice paper permeable to the light beyond them. The Archer listened intently, hearing soft whispers and the gentle laughter of women coming from behind the thin walls, which obscured his view. In the corner of the large room, a bow and a quiver of arrows leaned against one wall. He noticed a golden glow emanating from the quiver which stood alone. The Archer wondered about this but did not dare to touch what was not his.

Startled, the Archer looked up to find an Asian woman wearing a flowing white and gold dress. Her face was covered with white rice powder, setting off her almond eyes. He was astounded to see such beauty and taken off guard as she stood watching him. Bewildered, he stood to greet her, bowing. The woman then asked if her master was in need of anything. Without a word, he moved past her to the door beyond. His height was great, and he had to stoop in order to make his way to the outside. The Archer found himself standing in a garden of greens with many different hues of color. To his left was a pond where koi swam carefree and the surface was adorned with bouquets of floating lotus blossoms. Cascading water fell into the pond at the far end, breaking the silence as sweet ginger and herbal aromas drifted on the cool breeze fragrantly filling the air. Butterflies and dragonflies swarmed the garden, gently sucking the nectar from nearby flowers and even landing on his hand. Here, he felt safe and empowered, at home in the surroundings of his mind. Closing his eyes, he breathed in deeply, allowing chi to enter, bringing him to a deeper awareness, a oneness with the universe. The Archer longed to know who he had been and from what time and space these dreams manifested themselves. He was confused by being called master and did not understand why the beautiful Asian girl would speak to him in such a manner. He turned, and his eyes met hers. She was bewildered and had tears streaming down her face. Slowly, he walked toward her and stood gazing at her face. Reaching out, he gently held her hands, which hung limply at her side. Then, with the sleeve of his shirt, he began wiping her tears, cleaning her face of all its makeup. Underneath the covering of rice powder, he found the purity of luminescent skin, a flawless complexion. The warrior in him studied her like he would a manifesto. She looked at him with sadness and asked, "How could it be that you do not know me, Archer?" The exotic woman's eyes were of a golden brown, reminding him of the variegated coloration of his wooden bow. Her lashes were long, like black feathers. Staring, the Archer reached to the crown of her head and took from her hair two decorated hair-sticks of red cinnabar, which held it in place high upon her head. As the sticks dropped to the ground, her hair fell, reaching the lower part of her back.

*Flowing black silk,* he thought. Hypnotized, he placed his hands on her face, taking all of her in. The Archer focused on her mouth, which was small with perfectly shaped lips, full and inviting. He slowly moved closer, closing his eyes to meet her lips with his. Armin's heart pounded as he felt the warmth of her breath, the softness of her touch and savored the sweet smell of her skin. Her eyes fell to the ground as she stood up on her toes to meet his supple lips. For a long time, they played with gentle kisses. Pulling her closer, he enfolded her in his arms with great strength. Intuitively, he knew the body he held and the lips he now kissed were familiar to him. Looking into her eyes with his unyielding gaze, the Archer took her with a hunger he had not known before, melting them into one.

A falling rock splashed into the lake, waking him from his reverie. The Archer was disappointed at having been awakened, for at last, the answers were coming to him. He knew the young woman was no stranger to him and longed to go back into his daydream to complete what he had started. Somehow, there was no mistaking that the answer lay in that place and with the woman who cried for him.

Sudden cries from Silverhawk pulled the Archer back to the present moment. Daylight was beginning to dim, and it was time to move on. Heading to northern Germany, he would begin his trek on the path of romance.

## Chapter Eleven

# A New Beginning

Würzburg was not too far from the forest's glacial lake where Armin had spent the afternoon daydreaming. He had decided to stay at the Hotel Maritim, a grand hotel that sits on the River Main, a place recommended by his friends in Austria. A porter escorted Armin to his room, making certain that all his needs were met. From the upper floors, the views were extraordinarily breathtaking. His window view was of the Main, which was bordered by lush forests and small towns dotting the hillsides. Picturesque churches and hilltop castles told of Bavaria's fascinating history. Armin's love of architecture was appeased, as Würzburg seemed to be a museum filled with rare and magnificent sights. Below, outdoor gardens embellished the walkways and sitting areas, which were pleasing to his senses. The Maritim offered homemade foods in a buffet style. Armin, a vegetarian, passed over the many trays of meats, finding his way to a colorful variety of vegetables and homemade soups, which satisfied his hunger.

After dining, he returned to the comfort of his room, where he rested and then showered himself using fragrant herbal soaps that soothed his senses. Turning the faucets to a warm temperature, he directed the water to flow through the showerhead, allowing the pulsating jets to massage his aching body. There he stayed until the water began to cool. He grabbed a neatly rolled fluffy white towel from a shelf above him and wrapped it around his slender waist as he walked to the bedroom. Armin gladly found the comfort of a real bed inviting after spending so many nights on the forest floor. This night, he expected to sleep without the haunting dreams that seemed to find him only in wilderness areas.

Sitting on the edge of the bed, he took a booklet that told more of this modest-size town of 140,000 people from the nightstand. "Würzburg is compact," it read, "made for walking and having a peaceful ambience. It is an ancient place located halfway between Frankfurt and Nuremberg. The occupation of this territory dates back to the Bronze Age, and it is known to have been settled by the Celts." Armin found the rich history alluring, knowing he would rest well this first night. He read on, "Many of the town's ancient structures and monuments were damaged or destroyed during a British air raid in March of 1945. Würzburg still held the spirit of medieval days, never going too far in the modern stream of life. This village was the beginning of the Romantic Road, which was built in the 1950s. Its construction was an effort to boost tourism in Germany after World War II. At first, the road was mainly used by families of American soldiers stationed in Bavaria and Füssen. But soon, its popularity grew as the road ambled south through Rothenberg, Dinkelsbuhl, and Augsberg and onward to the south."

Armin's eyes grew tired from reading, and his vision began to blur as each word ran into the next. Relaxed, he slid between the sheets, allowing himself to fall limp onto the softness of the mattress. Closing his eyes, it took only a moment before he fell deep into the void of sleep.

The night was hushed, vacant of turbulent dreams and the watchful eyes of the beautiful Asian woman who had wept for him or of a vigilant, wide-eyed owl. It was a night of quiet slumber for the weary traveler.

Never would a morning pass when the Archer did not begin his day with the slow, graceful movements of Taijiquan, grounding him and giving him an abundance of chi, enough to carry him through his active days. With the new sunrise, he was refreshed and ready for his journey south. Armin was heading to Munich when a sudden urge changed his route toward Regensburg, which was only an hour out of his way. Traveling through Germany's picturesque countryside, Armin enjoyed seeing the sunflower fields reach out across the landscape, contrasting with the beauty of the clear azure sky as he made his way home. Unknown to him, this would ultimately be his last time there.

While in his hometown, Armin attended to responsibilities that awaited him; some concerned his past, while others spoke of new ideas in business. He and his friends spent time discussing the building of a foundation and were excited, as they planned the many archery ranges they would create for the good of those in Wudang. During moments of quiet meditation, Armin welcomed the tranquility that enveloped his entire being. It was in this place of mindlessness that his connection to the Source was at its strongest. That evening, while listening to the voice of his soul, he was directed to a place in the world that would need his expertise. Armin had heard of the many problems in Lebanon, of the young people in that country who were having severe alcohol problems because of the stress and trauma of war. He felt it imperative to write to several international schools in Lebanon seeking to live the experience of uncertainty in an unstable region of the world. The very next day, a post in the newspaper presented itself; it was an opportunity to teach archery and athletics at a school in the Far East. Armin decided the position suited him and submitted his résumé. After waiting weeks, he received his letter of acceptance. Knowing about a new country and its culture and the experience would benefit him in many ways. He was open to all of life and to anything that God put before him. Never did fear or doubt enter Armin's mind. In the days ahead, he rested quietly with the decision he had made and found nothing to refute his choice; his body was calm and his mind peaceful.

Days later, he made flight arrangements. He took only a few belongings with him. His departure was without fanfare as he said good-bye to those he left behind. The Munich airport was 126 kilometers away, time enough for him to rest his mind. There would be no thinking back on what he was leaving, nor would he ponder what was to come. He lived the very moment observing those around him, watching and listening. If he chose, he easily found his way to his center, blocking out everything as he merged with a level far beyond earth.

The airport was bustling with a multitude of stressed travelers, reminding him of rush-hour traffic. The cab pulled to the curb, and Armin paid his debt, gathered his belongings, and walked into a sea of travelers buying tickets and trying to find their proper gates for departure. After only a short time of waiting, an airline attendant announced over the intercom that his plane was now boarding.

Photo by Armin Hirmer

## Chapter Twelve

# The Far East

*I*t was August of that year when the Archer arrived in the beautiful city of Beirut, Lebanon, which sits on a peninsula extending westward into the Mediterranean Sea, some ninety-four kilometers north of the Lebanon-Israel border. He had arrived early in Beirut, wanting to familiarize himself with his new surroundings and neighbors before the commencement of the academic year. He found a flat on the first level; he was more comfortable being grounded to the earth. This place had an ocean view. Each morning, he could watch the rolling of the sea as he ate breakfast on its small patio. His neighbors were curious about the new tenant. Showing him kindness, they looked forward to getting to know him. Over time, they would learn from each other new customs and about their different countries. The Archer listened carefully as they told stories of their lives, past and present, and of their hopes for the future.

Each morning, from his patio, he gave thanks for the view of the sea and the energy he felt there. As usual, he followed his morning ritual of stretching to the relaxing forms of his favorite martial art, keeping his mind and body fit. He worked arduously on the school curriculum, planning an informative program for his students, as this would be their very first introduction to archery.

September's commencement of school came on quickly, and each morning, as the Archer left for work, he would greet his neighbor with a smile and wave. Ahmed was a man of many years; his face was lined with deep furrows, telling of his days in the sun. He planted colorful gardens, one of flowers to please the eyes and the other of fruits to appease the appetite. The old man took a liking to his new neighbor and always reciprocated the Archer's nod, adding his own smile of greeting. These gestures placed both men in a lighthearted mood to last the day, as each knew without words how to send feelings from the heart. Now in a country where the language was not at all familiar to him, the Archer welcomed the challenge to learn. Fortunately, he spoke three languages fluently and another four in part. When he was a child, he had simply watched, learning everything as time went along. Now, he observed closely, using hand gestures for his needs if he lacked the words. It wasn't long before his communication skills improved.

News of the Archer's coming preceded his arrival. As this first day of school began, the children rushed through the doors, excited to start a new year. They were anxious to meet their new teacher, who brought bows and arrows for the archery program. Among a sea of dark-skinned, black-haired, and brown-eyed children stood a foreigner with graying hair, whose looks were unfamiliar to them. His eyes were fascinating, as they had never seen the color blue among their own. The Archer's gentle speech and easy way made trust come easily. His first days were long and difficult, as many duties were assigned to him. Never complaining, he did the best he could to accomplish each given task. The children were eager to learn his way with the bow. He taught them about patience, focus, balance, strength, and inner peace. Beyond all else, he stressed that intuition and intent would matter the most in the end.

The faculty took their turns monitoring recess each day, which certainly brought on a different set of dynamics. The Archer needed to watch the body language of each student, making certain that no bullying took place. Having taught for many years, he was well aware of the possibilities for unwarranted aggression when groups of children were together. Such behavior reflected the fearful or insecure ego mind. The Archer knew that maturity and time for most would heal their warped sense of power. It does not matter where one lives in the world, as nowhere is immune to human nature. So it was that he watched with the eye of an eagle. If he saw the potential for an uncomfortable situation, he would deflect the negatively charged energy by diverting those involved to a challenge on the soccer field.

Beirut was a mere 299 kilometers from Syria, where the threat of war with Israel was always looming and nerves were perpetually on edge. Finding himself in the midst of impending danger, he realized there was no protection from the madness of the world. However, the Archer felt safe within his conviction that what would be would be and as God intended. Often, he would see in the eyes of those he met an uncertainty about their future, as political unrest was at its peak. It was horrid and unthinkable that anyone would have to concern him—or herself with the atrocities and pain that war could bring. During moments of contemplation, he tried to understand the minds of men but had difficulty doing so. The Archer knew that all things were in God's hands and ultimately, in the end, good would prevail no matter how man acted out his ego mind.

After long hours at work each day, the Archer would find his way to the beach. There, the sand stretched far into the distance, having no end in sight. He would sit for hours waiting for the sun to fall beneath the horizon. This day, he sat atop a rocky ledge, listening to the rhythm of the waves cascading onto the shore. Falling into a trance, he searched the waters' depths, looking to find a hint into his elusive past. With only the faintest aura of light left in the sky, he would walk, as he did every day, miles back to his flat. His furnishings were sparse; no pictures hung on the walls looking back at him. A lone secondhand guitar, which he had purchased, leaned against the hallway wall, and as always, his bow and arrows were nearby. After supper, he sat playing his guitar and singing to keep himself company. There were no modern conveniences to help pass his time—no television, stereo, or house phone. He never complained or became frustrated with his life in Beirut. Instead, he was focused on the abundance that surrounded him. Life was perfect when filled with simplicity and void of material attachments. He was in good health, doing what he loved, and living close to nature—all of which were at his choosing.

His days at school were arduous, and the hours seemed to grow longer every day. As his students got to know him better, they would seek the Archer out regarding things other than athletics or archery. He found himself guiding the children, giving lessons on the do's and don'ts and etiquette of life. What developed wasn't only a student-teacher relationship but one of respect and friendship.

The Archer spent most of his time off alone, walking the city streets, familiarizing himself with the local area. He found his way to the BCD (Beirut Central District), which was the hub of the country's vibrant financial, commercial, and administrative centers. Cobblestone streets with stone façade buildings stood among the eclectic architectural designs. He noticed a mixture of French, Venetian Gothic, and Arabesque styles. These sights brought a rebirth to his love of architecture. He discovered many of the villages outside the modern rebuilt structures remained worn and some city neighborhoods were dilapidated. While he was walking in the old neighborhoods, he noticed that smells of homemade foods filled the air, rousing his need to find a café. Not far away, he came upon the perfect place for a vegetarian meal. He sat for a late lunch of vegetables, satisfying his hunger, and drank fine tea, which soothed his thirst. Allowing his stomach to settle, he watched passersby come and go. Some would stroll along, while others ran as if late for their appointment somewhere. He often wondered why anyone would rush about, as time only arrived when it was supposed to.

When finished with lunch, he took to walking the old, dusty road, which led back to the sea. On the long stretch of beach, he met every rock that had a place along the shore, many of which he would sit upon as he commenced his daily celebration of the setting sun. Waves would send their cool, misty spray upon him, like the stroking of a hand. When only the smallest bit of light held to the sky, he would find his way back home. Others nearby who honored the day in the same way that he did would wave or offer him a ride to the village. He always refused politely, preferring to walk, strengthening his legs as he enjoyed the warm evening breeze on his face and the salty smell of the sea air that followed him.

Many nights, the Archer longed for sleep to overtake him and dreams to fill his head with all he longed to know. This night, he opened the windows, allowing the night air to stir the stillness of his flat. It was the night of the full moon, and from his window, he noticed Silverhawk flying near, cautioning him about the dreams to follow. As he lay in bed, the breezes cooled his body, relieving him from the heat of the day. Willingly, he surrendered to the softness of his bed, floating further into the depths of oblivion, where images of his past would easily find him. Void of all sounds, the blackness of sleep soon overcame him.

Dreams arrived swiftly with visions of thousands of blackbirds filling the sky as a tornado sweeping across the earth, its funnel reaching toward the heavens. A stampede of stallions running toward him came with fury. Refusing to turn away, Armin stood firm, determined to face whatever was to come. His eyes strained to see through the thick cloud of birds that obscured his view. His chest pounded as his restless legs became tangled in the sheets that now entwined him. Coming from every direction, horses bore riders dressed in flowing garments of red and gold, offset by polished metal chest plates. Long black braids flopped wildly beneath their ornate helmets. The Archer heard the clamor of swords in the distance and the simultaneous sounds of men screaming as urgent commands were shouted. From nowhere, a black stallion charged toward him, jolting him off his feet. He hit the ground with force and then rolled away looking up at a mass of shiny black muscle thundering past him. The rider was a madman, or so it seemed. He was the one in command, and only he was dressed in black. The shimmer of his chest plate and the leather on his forearms and lower legs contrasted with his attire. Armin thought him to be regal, a man of majesty, who rode with perfect precision, gracefully taking stride as he intuitively controlled the beast below him. The Archer pulled himself from the ground, staring at the vision before him. "Who are you? *Who the hell are you?*" he screamed. Thirty feet away, he watched the horse rear up and the rider draw his sword as the wind blew his robes high in the air. The Archer's heart quickened, unsure of the consequences he faced from the one who haunted him. The rider raced back, coming to an abrupt halt only feet from where the Archer stood. Again, the horse reared into the air, its long mane floating upward. The rider held tight as he was flung onto the neck of the beast. Suddenly, the

Archer was face-to-face with his vision. They glared into each other's eyes as if looking into one another's soul.

Bravely, the Archer shouted in a commanding voice, "Who are you? And why have you continued to come to me?" The warrior shouted back from his mount. Yet, his voice rolled out only guttural sounds that had no meaning. Bewildered, the Archer shouted, "What do you want with me?" Frustration grew between them. The warrior again hollered out, using words that seemed to be of an ancient Chinese dialect. As though, with the rage of the gods the warrior looked to the heavens, his eyes red and bulging. Raising his sword, he screamed out into the sky. His bellow echoed fiercely into the darkening abyss. Lightning cracked, and thunder roared; the horse whinnied, rearing himself onto his hind legs while his front hooves pawed franticly into the emptiness of the air. The Archer stood firm, not backing down, knowing his dream could not hurt him. A voice then came from the clouds in answer to the warrior's cry. The black beast danced around the Archer once more, prancing on his hind legs sending up clouds of swirling dust as he reared high into the air. Not once did the Archer turn his back to the warrior. Fearless, he continued to stand firm, defying the phantom image before him.

Great clouds swirled as the heavens rumbled, turning to shades of charcoal. A voice, as if from God himself, filled the sky. "I am your father!"
Pale and confused, the Archer stood bewildered, looking in awe at the warrior and the beast of such beauty.

He rebuked the warrior, refuting the words he heard. He shouted back, "You are *not* my father! My father is dead and not of Chinese descent. You are mistaken, Warrior. Leave me forever! Stop this madness."

Again, a voice of thunder spoke. "I see you have not changed, my son! How dare you talk to me in this way of disrespect? I am your father, and you are my son! I have searched all the heavens to find you. Soon, it will be time for you to return. Come with me now!" he demanded.

"No, I will not! I do not know you, Warrior!" the Archer hollered in a booming voice.

The phantom raised his voice once more. "You chose a different way, Qin. Because of the decision and choices you made, I fell from my position as a mighty warrior. I was one with great honor but humbled and broken in the loss of my only son. Once you had gone from all who loved you, I could no longer fight for the deities of the times, nor could I look another in his eyes with pride. I have only come now to tell you that I have always loved you, and in that love, I have come to respect the decisions you made in a time when no man dared to stand against the rules of the deity. I never understood until my own death how great a warrior you truly were. Your strength and bullheadedness was not of ego-mind. It was simply that you knew your own soul. You let no other man lead you; instead, you made your own decisions. You were strong and knew your heart. You lived in honor, showing the treasures of moderation, humility, and compassion. How could I have not recognized all that I taught you?" Thinking him a madman, Armin turned and ran like the wind to reach the hill beyond. He looked back to see the warrior riding high on the back of the beast calling out, "Qin Xi Cheng, you *are* my son!"

Reaching over to the bedside stand, the Archer hit the button silencing the blaring chatter of the morning news. He rolled over in the bed only to find the sheets wrapped tightly around him. Sweat beaded upon his face. His body shuddered as if the cold of winter had frozen him in place. Stumbling to the shower, he stood, letting the water wash all remnants of his nightmare away. After dressing, the Archer had a light breakfast as he sat on the patio staring out at the sea. Normally, Taijiquan movements came to him easily, yet this morning, as he tried to empty his mind, he was pulled back into his nightmare, seeing the face of the warrior. *No, not now!* He screamed in the silence of his mind. *Not ever!* Unable to continue with his usual ritual, he sipped the last of his oolong tea and collected himself.

At school, the Archer was greeted by his students with friendly smiles and taunting please from the boys asking him to engage in a short preschool game of soccer. He agreed, knowing the exercise would do all of them good. School went as usual, but the Archer was not his normal self this particular day. Periodically, he found his mind wandering back to the dream that had held him captive throughout the night. The morning passed quickly, and the bell rang for recess. Joining the children outside, he watched their every move. Some of the girls sat next to him on the staircase as they awaited the next bell calling them back to class. One young girl leaned her head against his arm, something not permissible in a school setting, but she did not seem to care. The Archer wondered at first if she was not feeling well and asked her about this, but she said no. Was she comforting him, or was she in need of comfort herself? Salina asked if she could tell him of her dream. Smiling, he agreed to listen, relieved by the lightheartedness her story might bring, hoping for a certain reprieve from his own disturbing dreams.

Salina was suddenly embarrassed; her eyes fell to the walkway, and her cheeks turned a pinkish red. The Archer's eyes followed her young face as she began to speak. Fumbling for words, she was determined to tell him of her dream. "Well, I know this will sound weird, but here goes," she said. "I dreamed I was a mermaid with a beautiful tail of many colors. My hair was very long and followed me like endless strands of seaweed. I was very happy living in the sea and had lots of friends there. You know? Sea creatures and starfish and stuff like that." The Archer smiled. In a whisper, she said, "But one day, from the deepest part of the ocean, a sea monster came to harm all of us and to steal me away into the deepest part of the ocean. I swam as fast as I could, trying hard to get away. Panicking, I raced like a dolphin. Coughing and choking, I gulped for air as I surged through the waves." Salina's voice quickened as she relived her nightmare. "It all seemed so real," she continued. "I was so afraid, and somehow, you came into my dream."

Armin looked surprised and asked, "Why me?"

She could not answer but then thought of it and said, "I know that you are good and that you would protect me. I trust you as a father." Continuing, she said, "In my dream, you were a great warrior, who carried a sword at your side. It glistened in the sun. You wore a quiver of arrows at your waist and held a bow in your hand. When the monster came above the water, you were there, floating in the air on the back of a white stallion. You raised your bow, taking careful aim, and then shot him with a golden arrow. The monster screamed, and then, with a powerful swish of his tail, he fell into the ocean, sending up waves as high as a mountain. 'He is dead! We are safe!' I hollered to my friends. We were happy you came to save us. As I turned from my friends to thank you, you had disappeared. I just wanted you to know that it was a good dream after all and you are my hero." Salina's face turned pale white as she looked at her coach, a bit embarrassed. "Well, you are the one who saved all the creatures of the sea, and best of all, you saved me."

The Archer answered her by saying, "Salina, your mind is powerful and can manifest whatever you desire; know this of all things. You will need to rely on that wisdom in time to come." With that, she smiled at him and headed back to class. The Archer sat mystified, wondering what she had truly seen in him. Did she tap into his dreams? Was she a sensitive one, a person of knowing? He was curious and knew the answer to his own questions. Not wanting to dwell on the possibilities, he chose, instead, to enjoy the innocence of a child's dream and be the hero. How was it that she knew of the warrior and the golden arrows?

He had revealed to no one the story of the warrior or of the golden arrows that were silently left behind upon his departures.

The school bell rang, and the Archer held the main door open for a few straggling students. The rest of his day was uneventful, and he found himself looking forward to the final bell. Soon enough, he stood on the sidewalk waving as he watched the children getting onto their buses, which would take them to the safety of their homes. The Archer began walking down the road toward his flat when a taxi driver, leaning against his cab, met him with a warm smile and greetings in Arabic. Turning, the Archer smiled and answered the man with the few words he knew in the man's native language. The driver was surprised and awakened to the kind words of greeting. Happily, he offered his apple. Hesitating for moment, the driver put his finger up as if to ask the stranger to wait a moment, and then reaching onto the seat of his cab, he pulled out cookies his wife had made that morning and generously offered the foreigner one more gift. The Archer was grateful for the friendships he had made in Beirut, appreciating each face that greeted him along his way. The small snack he ate brought to mind that he had no time for lunch that afternoon. Hungry, his stomach rumbled as he walked away looking for a restaurant where he might purchase a salad to hold him over until morning. Finding a small café, he sat outside under its green canopy, resting after his meal. Although tired from his day, he found a path leading him to the sea. Arriving at the beach, the Archer watched the pounding of the waves while he listened to the roar of the surf. He was still wondering about the dream that had taken hold of him and also about Salina's ability to know of things beyond this reality.

Seabirds pecked at the sand and squabbled over morsels of food left by beachgoers. For hours, Armin enjoyed looking upon the immensity of the ocean. From his perch on a cliff rock, he watched the early evening's light fade from the sky as darkness approached. A blanket of silence fell upon the seashore; no sounds of birds, of man, or of the civilized world disturbed the serenity of the evening. He heard only the lowly murmur of gentle ripples touching the shore. It was like the quieting of tuning musicians before the maestro raised his baton, taking one to the edge of his heart. And so it was that the sea commanded the same respect as the maestro, while the sun sank below the horizon. It was a perfect ending to another day.

# Chapter Thirteen

# Another Dark Night

Armin walked the dark, lonely road toward home, yet he didn't mind the desolate trek, feeling safe in his environment. Upon reaching his flat, he swung the door open to a burst of hot air rushing at him. From the darkened room, he slid his hand across the wall, feeling for the light switch. He flipped the switch up and down several times without results. It had been weeks now that Armin had been without electricity and this was yet another sweltering night for him to endure. His ongoing electrical problems had become the norm, so he made the best of it. Ahmed was kind enough to give Armin a car battery, which he connected to an extension cord with a light bulb. He hung it on the cabinets, giving him light in the kitchen area. After making a cup of tea on the gas stove, Armin welcomed a cold shower and then climbed into the comfort of his bed. There, he prepared papers and worked on drawings of logos he created for his archery line, but he could only work by candlelight in his bedroom. Many of his friends from around the world looked forward to their continued communication, and he did the best he could sending emails from his laptop with what little battery power he had left. This was his only means of communicating with the world outside of Lebanon. Although many parts of Beirut were modernized, he felt he was living in an impoverished apartment building. Interestingly, only he suffered the consequence of having no air-conditioning and only intermittent power during the day. By night, he was shut off entirely. Armin had always chosen to live simply, having little desire to know intimacy with modern technology. But here in this country, he found many essentials were missing, causing unpleasant discomfort for no particular reason, or so he thought. His neighbors all had electricity, and each of them worried over the problems that only he seemed to be having. He began to wonder if the administration at the school had something to do with his electrical problems, as they controlled the power in his building. There had been an issue between Armin and the school administration that was never resolved. It was obvious that the students had taken a liking to their new teacher and familiarity grew between them. Friendliness and touching of any kind were not allowed, and the school atmosphere was strict in their rules. Here was a man of ease and freedom. He was one of sharing and listening, always kind in his ways. Armin stood against the strict rules and principles that were brought to his attention, living in accordance with his own philosophies and convictions, knowing full well that the children desired to be treated as equals and to be shown love and caring in their learning environment.

Now as the school year went into spring, the temperatures began to soar to near 35 degrees Celsius during the days with no relief at night, and always, his apartment was humid and sweltering hot. Armin accepted these discomforts, without disdain at first, knowing it would not be forever, believing as he did that there was a reason for all that happened and a lesson to be learned with each life experience.

Opening the bedroom window, he welcomed any breeze that would give him relief. Exhausted from the day, Armin finally closed his eyes. Sleep did not come easily, as he was soaked in sweat, his room stifling. Only a cold wet washcloth brought him a little relief. Soon, his body twitched, and darkness sent him from this world to the next as he surrendered to the night. Almost immediately, visions began to appear, and Armin was now under the watchful eyes of the beautiful Asian woman floating like a white mist in the shape of a human form high above his bed.

Moving nearer to him, Lilian reached out and placed her long, slender finger on his face as she slowly followed each line, tracing the perfection she saw before her. Staring at his lips, she sent love through her finger as she followed their form, not missing one curve of his mouth, this mouth she knew so very well. Lilian closed her eyes, remembering how she had once drawn the lines and creases of his ears with her tender touch. Placing her mouth near his ear, she whispered in the gentleness of her voice, "I am with you always. You hold my heart and my love for all of time. Feel me. Feel me." Her voice pleaded for him to hear her words, which echoed the longing of her desires. All of a sudden,

Armin stirred, and his arms flailed wildly, as if to swat a fly. Lilian moved back toward the ceiling. Hovering, she continued to watch over her master until dawn called her back to a dimension far lost to the present time.

Upon his awakening, Armin's routine was the same. He showered again in icy-cold water, which snapped him back to reality. Drying himself off, he shivered as he looked long and inquisitively into the mirror. He touched his lips, as if the feeling of another's touch lingered there. Urgently, he tried to recall words placed somewhere near the surface of his mind, but his efforts proved futile, at least for the time being. Armin ate breakfast on his patio, where he stretched and greeted a new day. Then, gathering his belongings, he headed down the roadway leading to school. The early morning hours were quiet, and he enjoyed the fresh morning air and peaceful walk. He never planned into the future, allowing flow to have its way, bringing what life had in store. This morning, a verse from the Tao interrupted the peacefulness of his morning walk.

> *Heaven is eternal—the earth endures.*
> *Why do heaven and earth last forever?*
> *They do not live for themselves only.*
> *This is the secret of their durability.*
> *For this reason, the sage puts himself last*
> *And so ends up ahead.*
> *He stays a witness to life,*
> *So he endures.*

*Serve the needs of others,*
*And all your own needs will be fulfilled.*
*Through selfless action, fulfillment is attained.*

Verse # 7 Tao Te Ching

Armin felt it imperative to show all the students respect and admiration, so he made it his habit to arrive at school early each day. There he sat on the front steps of the school, looking out on a desolate playground, waiting to greet each student upon his or her arrival. That particular day, a group of boys who were troublemakers noted for acting out in class and disrupting those taking archery seriously arrived before all the others. They seemed unsure of the foreigner and often would question their coach's authority, seeming to be testing his ability to control them. Many times, Armin tried to gain their trust, by engaging them in an early morning game of soccer, an offer they gladly accepted. The group of rebels knew of Coach's expertise in the martial arts and tested his quick response that morning after their brief game of soccer, surprising him with an attack from behind. Armin met their challenge with the ease and the grace of a leopard. Each, in his own turn, found himself lying in the dirt, with only his dignity harmed. A new respect came from each of them, as they wanted to know more of Taijiquan and the swift moves and control it taught. Armin never refused, knowing each lesson would help them focus as they learned of intent. These lessons would change their lives once mastered, bringing each of them wisdom to last a lifetime. Armin then returned to the school steps. The grounds soon became crowded and chatter filled the morning air as welcoming smiles were exchanged.

School began as usual, and this day, the classes had moved outside where the sun and a cool breeze made for perfect shooting weather. The new day brought with it a settled feeling from the other students, who had felt a release of tension between their disruptive peers and Coach Armin. The insecure young men knew now that there was nothing to fear from their coach and only good things would come from the lessons he taught.

Even though his days were long and exhausting, Armin felt a sense of accomplishment and peacefulness, knowing the insecure boys had a new view of themselves. After leaving the school grounds, he would stop at a local café for coffee and then take his usual walk along the road to the beach. Friendly faces on those he met on his way eased any wandering thoughts he may have had. Armin was not one who took kindly to disruptive ways or strident rules, which reminded him of his own childhood days at school. So too, as a teacher, he found that the practices of the administrative officials were controlling and excessive. Ego mania ruled over attending students and faculty as well. This weighed heavily on his mind at times, as he never understood why men had a need for power. He knew well that actions such as these came from individuals who had low self-esteem and the inability to love themselves. They lived under false pretenses, believing they were more important than any other, a façade many hid behind. The Archer simply chose to let his thoughts go. He sat on a jetty quietly looking out to sea, watching the waves crest and fall to the shore. His mind was now empty except for the gratitude he held for the beauty of nature before him. Neither, the turmoil of his days nor any feelings of loneliness he had living in a new and foreign country seemed to matter. Armin always made the best of all by replenishing his soul, finding comfort in nature and his meditations. The last of the sun had fallen beyond the horizon, and only dim light from a rising moon lit his path home.

Photo by Armin Hirmer

Warm evening breezes still held moisture in the air, and Armin found himself longing for a shower and satisfying supper. Entering his flat, he flipped the wall switch mostly out of habit, hoping to find he had electricity. The room remained black. He tried the switch several more times, hoping it would only be a loose wire, but nothing. Armin could not help but wonder why he was the only tenant in the apartment building who had no electricity. Could it be the pending war between Syria and Israel and a need to conserve energy? Or perhaps it was only the malicious behavior of another? He did not know any of these answers and laid the questions to rest.

Hearing his stomach rumbling, he felt for the car battery. Connecting the wires, he hung the single bulb from the cabinet, giving him enough light to move about his flat. After finishing his supper of vegetables, he lit a few candles and then showered in freezing-cold water, cleaning the salt from his body. Refreshed, he slid between his sheets. The archery manuals he was working on had to wait for yet another day. With no air-conditioning to cool the stagnant air of his flat, Armin began to feel his living conditions were more suited for one imprisoned within an environment controlled by another. He lay contemplating his service at the school, recognizing the discontentment he was beginning to feel. Daily, one more job was added to his signed contract, one more constriction to the use of his archery field, one more discipline in his work with the children. He knew he would finish out the year, honoring his contract. Admittedly, there were days when he wondered if he were doing the right thing. He gave the children his very best, teaching them of love, understanding, patience, tolerance, and expertise with the bow. As the end of the school year approached, Armin still questioned his decision to move to the Far East. He trusted that God had a lesson for him to learn in the choosing of this assignment. As time went on in this place, he did much good, and the children learned many things. He saw firsthand the changes in them as knowledge and maturity came to each of them. Armin's thoughts were fading as his eyes closed. Still, his dreams would spark and flit away. He was unable to capture the complete story of his intricate mind but felt a presence with him, one he had never sensed so strongly before. This brought him comfort, after having been pulled so far out of alignment.

With June's arrival, the school year approached its end. Civil unrest in the city brought officials at the school to let the graduating students leave two weeks ahead of the scheduled end of the year. Armin's contract ran through to the end of the summer, yet he yearned for an early departure. Talk of war was on the rise, and Syria was taking position to begin bombing Israel. These threats placed the entire country on high alert, leaving its citizens uncertain of their fate to come. Near the end of June, Armin approached the administration of the school requesting an early dismissal from his contract. He was told that he could leave but would be denied any money due him through August, so he chose to stay on, even under worsening conditions and the suffocating heat of the summer months.

In early August of 2012, Armin awaited the end of his school year. Talk of war between Syria and Israel had escalated. A heavy police presence was revealed as unease and uncertainty crept in like a misty cloud, hovering over all of Lebanon. Armin still walked the city streets and even enjoyed his evening mocha at Starbucks in downtown Beirut until the early evening hours sent him on his way. He boarded the bus taking him to the outskirts of the city and finally to the safety of his flat. The shrill sounds of blaring ambulance sirens and police vehicles raced to an emergent situation. Once home, he called a friend from his mobile phone. She informed him of what she knew regarding the incident and noises coming from the distance. Unbeknownst to Armin, a sniper had shot a Sunni sheikh in a downtown district in Beirut in the exact spot he had been awaiting his bus only fifteen minutes earlier. After finishing his call, Armin and his neighbors watched from the rooftops as those filled with outrage retaliated by setting off firebombs in protest. Vehicles were overturned and stores damaged as the carnage lasted for days. Even school had been canceled during this time, and once again, life was interrupted by the egos of men.

Photo by Armin Hirmer

There was nothing to be done through August, seeing that the entire cleanup at the school had already been completed. Each teacher was remanded to work in an old musty library filled with the smell of ancient moldy books piled high. The small, one-room library, with little lighting, was crammed. Old wooden shelves were sagging with outdated manuscripts waiting to be counted and logged. There were no barcodes or electronic means by which to catalog the thousands of books. Instead, it was demanded that all be done one by one at the teachers' hands. Armin thought it ridiculous, again feeling the constraints of binding walls around him. The provoking silent aggression of those in control only strengthened his devotion and commitment to living the Way of the Tao. Further, it was teaching him patience, compassion, and acceptance. It was not a punishment bestowed upon him, as one might think, but instead a lesson. He now knew the reason he had been guided to the unstable region of the world.

His final days in Beirut found Armin watching the calming waters of the sea as he looked for a sign of his next calling. On the fourth day, he heard the urgent call of Silverhawk long before he saw the great bird. Armin smiled, knowing the time had come for him to move on.

Over the next few days, the Archer made certain to say good-bye to all those who had made a difference in his life. One student in particular with whom he had made a connection came to mind. Sishiba had an ancient soul and wisdom far beyond her years, leaving him to wonder if they had not known one another in a past time. They had spoken often outside at recess where she would reveal her dreams to him, describing flowing gowns of silk, majestic horses stampeding the land, and men with clanking swords seeming to be in battle. He looked at her in awe as he wondered where all this had come from. For how could she know the same visions of his dreams? She told of specific details connected to the visions that haunted him, those he would never dare mention to anyone. Her intuition painted pictures upon the canvas of her mind in the darkness each night. In silence, the Archer concluded that Sishiba did hear and see the mystical dreams of others. He knew she was connected to her Source, and with this, her intuitiveness was opened to the entire universe. Salina, who was a friend of Sishiba, also had the gift of insight. Salina had heard the news of the Archer's leaving as well and was saddened to know that her hero from the sea would soon be gone. Each night, she cried, anticipating the loss of her teacher and friend. The Archer was approached by Salina's mother who told him of her daughter's distress at his leaving. He knew that several hours on the archery field would help both the girls through this difficult time, bringing them peace in his departure. So the targets were set, bows drawn, and arrows launched throughout their last time together, bringing all of them delight and a bonding of spirits. The Archer knew the young women would do well in their lives, as would each of the students he taught. The girls thanked Coach Armin for his time. Walking away, Sishiba turned and asked for one more session the following day, her last with her teacher and the bow.

For the few days that followed, Sishiba would walk past the field looking for the Archer, yet he did not return. In her sadness, she walked toward the lone target that sat at one end of the field, and there, a glistening caught her eye. As she came closer, she noticed it was a golden arrow, much like the one held by the vision of the man in silk riding on the back of a black stallion. Had her nightmares followed her into reality? She found herself questioning what was before her, asking how this could be. Had the coach made this arrow especially for her, or was this a manifestation of her own intuitive mind? Taking the arrow from the target, Sishiba smiled knowing that at least she had a part of her favorite teacher and friend. She noticed writing on the side of the arrow and knew this was not at all by chance. The message was surely meant for her. "Awareness and insight bring great wisdom; help those in need," it read.

Photo by Armin Hirmer

# Chapter Fourteen

# Mallorca

As the days flew by, Armin took care of his remaining business before departing. He made certain to visit friends with whom he had made a connection while in Beirut one last time. He walked forward, aware that his tomorrows would bring another task and newness to his life; more teaching would create a horizon of giving. In the flat, he left behind the guitar that had kept him company for the past year. Playing his instrument stirred his soul, taking him away from the reality he lived in the absence of simple comforts and bringing him pleasure. Armin's bow and quiver of arrows stood against the wall. These he would leave behind for the next tenant to discover. The wood carried Armin's spirit, and the new owner would feel his lasting energy.

A voice within directed him to his next destination, an island. Armin loved the warmth of the sun and tropical temperatures that would care well for his aching bones. For in his eyes, the tranquility of the sea soothed his soul. Within the rolling of the waves, he could see the past coming closer. And in this, awareness of from where he truly came would solve the question of the dreams that haunted him, a revealing of his ego mind. There, he would watch the rising of the moon and the setting of the sun, which seemed so close that if he reached out far enough into the sky, he could touch them. These were things of his heart. Often he would place his finger in the sea and his spirit would find the soul of another who lived far across the world from him. On this last visit to the shore, Armin looked at his reflection in the water. There, a face gradually began to unmask itself in the ripples of the waves. It gave him a sense of familiarity. High cheekbones and almond-shaped eyes stared back at him, taking Armin's mind to a place from times long past. Yet the puzzle pieces were too obscure to remember each and every detail. Mysteries to unravel still lingered. He did not rush the coming of the stories of his mind, for he knew when the Great One was ready, so would be the answers he longed for.

Stepping from his dwelling place, he carried only one small suitcase that held his meager belongings. While waiting for his ride to the airport, Armin glanced once more at Ahmed's beautiful gardens. Appearing from nowhere, Silverhawk cried out; coming close, he fluttered his wings as if to stir the hair on Armin's head. The archer reached his arm out into the sky, and the bird passed near enough for the Archer to graze his fingers over his spirit guide's feathered body, affirming the binding of their souls. For the first time, Armin felt a new strength in their connection, one he had not felt before. His mouth began to move and words came out without warning. "Hooded Falcon," he said, grimacing, as he wondered why those words so easily flowed from him. A sudden apparition appeared before him. As he looked up the hill, the Great Warrior stared down upon him. He was mounted on a white stallion and appeared to be as big as life itself. The warrior's left hand and forearm were covered with a leather gauntlet and perched upon his arm was a hooded falcon, known for its hunting abilities and kept by noblemen and warriors. The warrior removed the hood from the bird, and there stood Silverhawk, regal on his perch. He stared into the eye of the Archer with intensity. Awed, Armin recognized himself from ancient times. Was this truly a vision of himself? He questioned it momentarily, but somehow, he knew the truth. Armin then flashed back to Salina and her dream of the white stallion upon which he rode when he slayed the sea monster. "Who is she? How did she know of me?" he asked out loud.

Impatiently, the taxi driver tooted his horn, breaking Armin's concentration. The vision before him fell to the ground like dust. He turned and walked to the waiting cab, looking back several times to see if he could find remnants of his vision lingering behind. The Archer's forty-five-minute ride to the airport brought back the many memories from his troublesome times in Beirut. He did not ponder the past but, instead, focused on the delight the children had brought him and the truths they each learned about themselves on the journey of their lives.

At night, visions and dreams had been his constant friend. He felt now a past love near him, one who stayed by his side each night while he slept. Armin could not help but wonder if these same dreams would continue to follow him to his new destination far away over many miles of ocean. His thoughts allowed his ride to the airport to go quickly.

Shortly, his destination was in view. At the curbside, he grabbed his suitcase and paid the driver, the very same man who had kindly shared his apple and his wife's homemade cookies. The Archer was so caught up in his last thoughts of Beirut that he never really looked at the driver. They smiled at one another, shook hands, and bid each other farewell.

The plane easily found its way into the open sky where he felt safer than he had on the soil of Lebanon, a country in the midst of uncertainty. The first signs of unrest in the region commenced only weeks before Armin's departure. Fires continued to be set in the city streets, and now the tanks rolled in taking position in wait of the first move by the opposition. *It seemed that Syria's hatred had overflowed into peaceful Lebanon*, and of this, Armin wanted no part. He was grateful to be on his way enjoying the views below. He watched as fishermen filled their bobbing vessels with a hardy day's catch. A good harvest brought security to families depending on the sea for their livelihood. As he always did when leaving a place, he felt sadness within, but he closed his eyes, making the thoughts flee and melting his mind into emptiness. Moments later, he found himself looking out the window once again, at a sky of blue and white billowing clouds lining the heavens.

Armin's journey to Mallorca would be very long. This beautiful island was located in the Mediterranean Sea. It was the largest of the Balearic Islands, which belonged to Spain. During his flight, he worked on his archery manual, for which he had many new ideas. Using his gift of drawing, he designed new logos for his business and worked on his booklets of improved archery techniques. This occupied his time, never permitting him to fall asleep, as he denied himself that luxury whenever he flew. After many hours, he looked out the window and saw in the distance a speck on the vast ocean. As the plane approached the island, she showed her green landscape and majestic mountains. Beaches white with sand encircled the entire island, looking from the sky like the ring of an archer's target. The pilot soon announced their estimated time of arrival, and a swell of excitement ran through the passengers seated around him. The island was a place that knew him well. Many years earlier, he had established a business for the sport of archery there, one which had sustained itself during his long periods of absence. This had once been his home, and here, he felt a sense of belonging. Familiar with his surroundings and a friend to the locals, Armin could relax, feeling free. He couldn't wait for his feet to hit the ground. Soon, the plane taxied onto the runway and finally came to a stop. He gathered his belongings then disembarked the aircraft and immediately took a taxi to his place of work.

The island of Mallorca was a paradise for vacationers, who came from around the globe to enjoy the many amenities the island had to offer. Approximately eight million tourists invaded Mallorca during peak season each year. Hospitality was the focus at any one of the large resorts that sat directly on the coastline. Here, advanced practitioners and novices in the sport of archery could learn to perfect their skills. They learned how to make their own bows and arrows. Young and old alike partook in the shaving of the wood and bending of the bows into shapes they preferred. There was laughter and joy in the creating process, and exhilaration rang out when the arrows flew and hit their marks. People came to learn Taijiquan, finding inner silence and peace as they practiced the ancient art form for gathering their chi. Many of the guests came seeking to become one with themselves and ultimately, one with the universe. Here, empty minds flowed like water with graceful beauty and ease.

Armin chose to live more simply, away from the fanfare and the noisy confusion of resort life. A small but comfortable hut awaited him on the hillside above the hotel. This was the place he called home. There, away from the beach areas, he found solace in the rolling of the hills and mountains that overlooked the sea. He took his work seriously, as he did wherever he was in his world of travel. He would teach not only about the bow but about many things that connected the mind, body, and spirit. He used the philosophy of the Tao and its vital wisdom, which he shared with his many students. In the end, he proliferated the meaning of love and the true knowing of one's place in the world. When Armin centered himself, as he did using meditation, his soul connected to the universe, opening his mind to knowing and intuition.

"We are here to give all of ourselves for
the greater good of those we serve."

—Unknown

# Chapter Fifteen

## The Pez Espada

The Hotel Pez Espada was grand and sat in a sea of emerald greens and variegated hues of turquoise, all which were mesmerizing to the eye. The hotel had frescos matching the likes of Leonardo da Vinci's extraordinary works. It offered a flare of elegance, having cathedral-style ceilings, with pools both inside and out. There were workout rooms with instructors for each guest's every desire. The hotel's appeal was endless, and many were interested in the archery program. Armin found his way by taxi from the airport and immediately went to the range where he met many of his old friends and those who taught in his absence. After all the excitement of his welcome home, he went to the range and began to teach. A small group had gathered for the afternoon archery session, and he began by letting each of them get used to the feeling of the bow, finding comfort with it. Needing to relax his students, he then taught them about proper breathing, using only the nose to execute his technique. "Relax with the breath, push the belly outward on inspiration, and then let yourself go. Relax," he would say.

Nita, his friend of many years, did not know of his return, as Armin never divulged when he came or went. Smiling and shaking her head, she just leaned against the archery tent and watched with delight as Armin and several other instructors began their sessions. Each day, he found new students signing up for classes; many were shy and uncertain of their ability to shoot, but soon, their nervousness would end and confidence would abound.

Armin continued, "Spread your feet to match the width of your shoulders. Pretend that you are standing on railroad tracks. Now bend your knees slightly, bowing the knees out as if riding a horse. Your body weight is centered between both of your feet. Relax in this position, and just breathe. Allow yourself to become centered. Imagine roots growing from your feet deep into Mother Earth as you ground yourselves. Twist only your heads, and look to the mark. You are now at a ninety-degree angle from your target." Armin handed each newcomer a bow and let them get use to holding it, feeling the wood until they were comfortable. Next he had them pluck the bow string pretending to have an arrow in the nock. He asked them to raise the bow having each pull the string back so their middle finger would rest at their lip. Each student used the traditional style of shoot using three fingers on the string. They re-enacted the movements until comfortable. Armin continued guiding each new student as he felt comfort in his return to Mallorca

A sudden disturbance took Nita from her resting position. A young lady, in the archery class removed herself from the crowd and sat beneath a palm. She watched the others with great interest but she was weak and summoned Nita to the palm shaded table with a simple lift of her hand.

Nita stood looking at this dark-haired beauty, realizing she was not feeling well at all. Her face, although tan, was pale, and her eyes had difficulty staying open. Immediately, Nita brought a tall glass of cool water, making the young woman sip gently on the straw. She was like a wilted flower being watered; soon, the young beauty began to come back to life as she rehydrated herself. She was still in need of care, so Nita was compelled to stay with the young woman, who, after some time, extended her hand. "My name is Giovanna. I thank you so very much for your help." She then motioned Nita to sit beside her.

Thinking twice of this, Nita realized she had other responsibilities to tend to. Recognizing, however, that the young woman remained weak and seemingly in need of company, she decided to stay watching Giovanna's continued recovery. The two began speaking to one another, sharing stories. Giovanna asked questions of Nita as to why she worked in the hotel and did not choose to educate herself properly. She suggested that Nita at least apply for a position of higher status that would pay her more money. Surprised at such personal questions, Nita said little. She just smiled, turning the focus back on Giovanna. During their conversation, Nita learned that the young woman was from Italy and came to Mallorca with her father, a widower who often visited the island doing business with many of its shopkeepers in nearby cities and villages. Giovanna went on to tell of her loneliness since the death of her mother and the overbearing protection of her father. Nita felt the sadness that overwhelmed Giovanna and thought it best to divert her attention to something more enjoyable. She knew all the while that the Archer had a way about him, a way with words that would soothe Giovanna, allowing her to find peace. Armin would understand the anguish she felt in the death of her beloved mother and her father's new concerns and interference in her life. Nita pointed to the archery range suggesting she return to class.

Giovanna looked in the direction of the beach, where all the targets were set up with the sea as a background. She noticed another instructor with graying hair who could not miss the target. Turning to Nita, she asked who this man with such control and accuracy was. Nita smiled and said, "He is my friend. He is the Archer and will teach you, if you choose to study." Giovanna continued to ask more questions about this man as they walked toward where he stood. Nita turned and said, "All you need to know of him is that he can easily calm the madness that often haunts a personality. He makes sense of the insensible. The Archer will observe and oftentimes not speak at all, for within the silence, he speaks a million words. He will teach you many things, for in the circle of giving is the completion of loving, as you will soon see." Giovanna looked at Nita questioningly as she contorted her face in wonder at what she had been told. With this, Nita's eyes directed Giovanna to look upon the Archer. She introduced the two. In turn, Nita said, "You are now where you need to be. Armin will take good care of you and teach you the way of the bow." Nita looked Armin in the eyes, and without an exchange of words, he knew what she was saying and smiled at her, nodding his head. Nita turned to leave the range and looked back at Giovanna, saying, "Enjoy your time with the Archer." She added, "Oh yes, to answer your question, Giovanna, I have taken the footsteps of my father. I am the daughter of the owner of the Pez Espada."

Embarrassed, Giovanna bowed her head and gave a simple blush, followed by a grateful, "Thank you."

Armin worked with the young woman until dusk settled over the sea. Giovanna's father came to retrieve her from the teachings of the Archer. The men greeted one another, and Roberto Centrino thanked Armin for his time and kindness to his daughter. Turning to walk away, the Archer could hear the excitement in Giovanna's voice as she told her father of her day learning archery and all that had awakened within her. She pleaded with her father, asking for permission to return the next day for more lessons. Armin knew from the sound of her voice that he would surely see her again. With this, Armin cleared the range of left-behind arrows and straightened some of the targets. He picked up several shirts lying on the ground and other garments left behind by careless guests. Then, he headed back to the archery shop where he placed the items in the lost and found. Turning the sign on the door to read "Closed," he made sure all was in its proper place before shutting out the lights. Picking up his black suitcase, he headed up the long sandy path leading to his mountain hideaway.

Nita, her father, and the staff were excited to have Armin back on the island and were especially appreciative of his dedication. He had worked his first day back on Mallorca. Nita knew how Armin liked his home to be and sent staff to prepare the dwelling prior to his arrival up the hillside that day. The hut had been unoccupied for a very long time and was musty. They opened the door and windows to air the place out and then swept the floors and cleaned as best they could. Bowls of colorful vegetables, fruit, teas, and coffee, all to his liking, were placed on the counter along with fresh herbs placed nearby to freshen the smell inside. She also knew of his love for music and brought her spare guitar to keep him company. Knowing he preferred to be as close to nature as possible, they arranged his bed to be outside of his small but comfortable cabana-style hut.

Armin's long flight and the wind off the sea, although warm, had taken a toll on him, and at day's end, he found himself exhausted. As the sun set in the west, he relaxed with movements of Taijiquan and gazed out upon the vastness of the aqua sea. That evening, he enjoyed his last mocha of the day. Armin then sat listening to the sounds of crickets and the chatter of small animals, who added their voices to the night's symphony. Soothing sounds of life all around readied him for a restful sleep. Cascades of white netting blew gently in the evening breeze and surrounded the hammock, which hung in between two tall palms, lending shade for his eyes from the early morning sun.

The Archer's first week on the island did not push aside the dreams that seemed to follow him. The hauntings that he so desperately needed to understand weighed on his mind, and he felt their presence to be near. The passing of Silverhawk in the distance warned him of a stirring in the air and restlessness in the atmosphere, a sure sign of the coming of yet another vision or entity from his elusive past. Before sleep overtook him, he lay there, thinking casually of the day to follow, when suddenly, the piercing cries of Silverhawk came nearer, blending the symphonic sounds of the night. There, only feet from his sleeping place, the great bird landed and nestled himself on an island palm. They eyed one another by lantern lights and the torches that surrounded the hut. Armin looked deep into the yellow of the bird's eye; neither pulled away from the other's stare. He knew then, beyond all doubt, there would be the coming of another dream.

# Chapter Sixteen

## Lilian's Visit

The gentle rocking motion of Armin's hammock lulled him, like a mother as she offers her child to the peace of the night. Mesmerized, he found sleep with ease, and he drifted from this plane. In a short while, his sleep was disturbed by the presence of an entity that floated above where he lay. An Asian woman of great beauty wore a white flowing dress that moved easily with the stirring of the breeze. As she watched his every breath, Armin fluttered his eyes, sensing her presence, in a brief moment he gazed upon her face, only for her to turn from him. The billowing white fabric of her dress revealed the perfect curves of her body, and he viewed her soft, milky skin beneath. Armin remained motionless, paralyzed in the sleep stage of REM where dreams occur. He wanted to face her, as he had the warrior, to learn of all that she could reveal to him. His thoughts called out, asking her to turn her head so that his eyes again could rest upon her face. Summoned by telepathy, Lilian turned. Armin looked deep into her almond-shaped eyes, which twinkled in the light, turning them to soft brown. Studying her face, he realized she was beyond captivating. High cheekbones sat evenly at each side of her face like fine pieces of artwork, each framed by her long jet-black hair, which hung down her back blowing gently in wavy lines to match the movements of her flowing dress. Sparkling in the torchlight, tears began to fall like soft drops of rain. He felt her sensitivity and struggled to get words to flow but could not.

They were still connected. Lilian knew his every thought. She had waited an eternity to find him, as her love had never faded through all the ages. So desperately, she wanted to lie beside him holding him close. Then and only then, could she smell his skin and feel the goose bumps rise as she touched his body, whispering of her love and the fullness of her heart. Knowing that for now, her desires must be set aside; Lilian would wait, for all things had a time of happening. She longed only for the moment he would finally know the truth and be free.

Slowly, she began to tell him what his heart needed to know. Her eyes fell upon him, and tears began to clutch her cheeks as she spoke. "I have watched you sleep every night since the beginning of your life here. Yet you have not felt my presence and do not recognize me even now, yet I have always been with you. There was a time, Archer, when you knew my touch. You have also known the softness of my mouth." Overwhelmed in his presence, she hung her head and wiped her face gently, remembering times of long ago.

Armin again struggled to speak, wanting to tell her he was beginning to see dreams in his mind, remembering fleeting moments of their time together, yet much was still vague. The sound of her voice stirred emotions in him and brought images to life, images that had been dead for many ages.

Lilian's voice was soft, blending into the harmony of sounds beyond the flowing nets that surrounded her. As she looked at him, her lips began to tremble and words flowed once more. "Centuries ago, in the great land of China, when wars were fought and dynasties were built, we shared a perfect love." Her head fell as she collected her thoughts and held back the many emotions that wanted to explode in that moment. Her insides were screaming with wonder, asking herself if she was alone in the loving of him. Then she remembered her true heart, knowing love unreturned had its own rainbow as well.

"It was the year 1600 BC in the province of Henan, at that time the capital of China. We were then of the Xia Dynasty, the first and oldest in the land. Our fathers were farmers. Our farms were small but fruitful, producing enough to feed the many. They were sought out by the government to become bow makers, as it was in your family's history to produce the greatest bows in the lands." Looking at Armin, Lilian searched for any sign of familiarity. She added, "Our fathers were bowyers for the emperor's armies during that time. Do you remember?" she asked. "We were neighbors in our teens then, and this is how I came to know you." Lilian looked at him, hoping for some sign of recognition or remembrance from Armin, but there was nothing. She continued, "When I first saw you, my heart would pulsate and my stomach turn with great excitement as I could barely look at your face. You were gentle with me and made me laugh to get over my shyness. Soon enough, I could look at you without blushing, and in time, I stopped nervously stumbling and dropping things in your presence. Our parents knew of our feelings but said nothing. Their facial expressions revealed happiness and approval of our relationship. Qin, you would take me to the fields of high grass and would teach me to shoot the arrows. You taught me to love and respect the bow, and I would watch you empty your mind, trying to do as you did. You always told me to accept all things as they came and never to ask the why of it but to live only in the moment that time presented. You became my teacher and instructed me in all the things that warriors studied. I learned from you about all the elements—fire, earth, metal, water, and wood—and how they intermingled with all of life making for perfect flow. You were proud of me as I mastered all so quickly, becoming one with the bow. We rode our horses together, shooting at the targets many times, and we pretended to fight with swords, just as your father had trained you to do in preparation for your days as a mighty warrior. He groomed you well, and, in turn, I knew most of what you were taught as you generously shared your every secret. When tired of the games we played, we would lie in the high grass, hiding from the world. There, we watched the koi swim in a hidden pond that only we knew existed. For hours, we would watch the pond, which lay near the foot of a small mountain range, where streams were plenty and the subtleties of nature were filled with wonder. Our days were consumed with laughter, and our hearts were full of light and the joy love brought. Never could I have had enough of you."

Lilian cast her eyes to the hammock where Armin lay and stopped speaking, catching her breath for a moment. She reminded him that they had met earlier in his dreams, in the garden of her parents' home. "There, I asked you, Qin, 'Does my master need anything?' Your eyes only looked through me then. I realized in that moment you did not know me. I followed you to the outside garden, our favorite place, and you watched the koi and listened to dancing sounds of water trickling into the pond. Often, in quiet moments, we would go there and sit for hours saying not one word, just listening to all around us. In silence, you were whole, and in the wholeness of being, you spoke a million words, yet never did my ears hear a murmur from your lips."

Armin looked startled, wanting to ask her about the name she had called him. This name was the same used by the phantom warrior who called him "son." She continued, "You looked at me with uncertainty. Looking into my eyes, you began to wipe off my painted face, gently kissing my lips. I thought you remembered." Armin's eyes gazed upon her, desperate to tell her he was beginning to feel all that had been placed in a box locked somewhere inside of his heart. He remained frozen in his dream state, unable to move or communicate.

Lilian felt his frustration and then quickly collected herself, saying, "Trained by your father and others, you became a great warrior. You knew the way of the sword and rode horses as you shot the bow in times of battle. Never were you one to fight, Qin; this was not your belief. One day, you simply vanished forever. Some say you fled because you would not fight for the cause of the government. They believed you possessed too much fear to be a true warrior, yet I knew better. Your heart had no fear, and I trusted your reason for leaving. You were always strong-minded, and never did I know you to take another man's word for what you did not believe. True warriors are not made by men; instead, they are born from roots of the heavens and earth with a godly knowing of integrity, honor, and compassion for all of life. Each experience is a labor of love, ever reaching toward that higher reward."

> *"Knowing others is wisdom; knowing yourself is enlightenment."*
> —*Lao Tzu*

"You were a different spirit, one who had confidence in all you did, and strong of mind like none other. I understood you! In time, many soldiers came looking for you, thinking you were near me. They searched everywhere, determined to find and imprison you. They kept a watchful eye on me as well, for a long time. Militants were certain you would come back. Yet never did you return. One night in the darkness and cold bleakness of a winter storm, they took me from my father's house, thinking they could make me talk, wanting me to reveal where you were. I did not know, as you wanted it to be. They were forceful and cruel, depriving me of basic essentials, questioning me for days, hoping I would break my silence and tell them what they wanted to know. My life was difficult. I worked menial jobs, scrubbing floors and washing walls until my knees were bleeding and bruised. Eventually, I worked outside as a laborer, plowing and planting fields. I had little food for myself and was kept away from the others in solitude. I lived a difficult life at the hands of the government. I was fading into nothingness; my heart was heavy with sorrow, and the terms of my life were not for those of living souls. Now I float as one with the universe, free, still loving you as I had in the very beginning." Armin's thoughts could not grasp the reason for this. His mind longed to know why such severity was taken by the hands of the government. This made no sense to him. "You fought against the government alongside the commoners to hold what little property and livestock we owned. You were a Robin Hood for the poor and discarded by those in control. They feared you, Archer!" Lilian said. She reached down to touch his face, and he felt the warmth of her hand going through him like a lightning rod.

The stirring of the wind and the cawing of Silverhawk awakened the Archer from his dream state. He looked about, hoping to see the image of Lilian, but she was gone. Armin found himself wondering if she had really ever been there at all. Slowly, his paralytic state lifted and he made his way inside the hut. There, he splashed water on his face and held it cupped in his hands over his eyes, hoping this would bring him back to reality.

Armin prepared for the day ahead, thinking back on his night of visions, surprised that he remembered and felt something from the past. Yet, in this experience, he was amazed that somehow, he felt great comfort. Armin made his morning coffee and then stepped outside looking over the sea. Planting his feet firmly on the earth, he felt the wind touch his face; he was grounded in the here and now. "*Now* is all that matters," he said to himself and then placed his thoughts behind him.

# Chapter Seventeen

# Giovanna's Story

O vertired from his long night of visions, Armin's rest had teetered on the brink of sleeplessness. He often found himself drifting back, longing to see Lilian and to hear her voice, a voice that had spoken words to settle his mind and others that would settle the riddles of his life and open a window to his past.

A bright sun hung in a cloudless sky, illuminating the island. From the privacy of Armin's hilltop hideaway, he watched as guests gathered below, filling the range. His day was obviously planned, and he was happy that his teaching schedule was full.

Arriving at the range, Armin found a large group of enthusiastic students awaiting his arrival. There were some with experience in shooting and others who had never held a bow. He began his teaching with the basics of breathing, stance, body posture, and grounding himself. He again allowed each of them to first hold the bow and get used to the feeling of it so they would be comfortable and relaxed. They practiced pulling the string without arrows, making certain the draw weight was right for each of them. Some arms flew wildly as the students released the string, and Armin then corrected them, demonstrating the release was in the fingers not in the arm.

At noon, Armin took a break from his teaching and wandered out to his favorite spot on a rocky cliff overlooking the Mediterranean Sea. He enjoyed a light lunch as he watched the seabirds glide on invisible air currents. All of nature surrounded him as he sat perched high above the churning turquoise waters below. The warm noonday sun soothed the stiffness in his muscles brought upon him by the many hours he lay motionless, in the paralyzing sleep state of REM, a state that kept him captive throughout the night. Suddenly, the rocky ledge beneath Armin began to shake as he heard the thunderous pounding of hooves in the distance coming nearer. His head began to vibrate as he felt the earth beneath him tremor. At first, he feared that a quake was beginning to erupt, a stirring in the belly of Mother Earth. Armin stopped, thinking again it was his dreams following him into an awakened state. Searching the sky for Silverhawk, he did not understand why there was no warning given him.

A noisy commotion arose behind him. Turning, he looked over his right shoulder in the direction of the hill beyond the archery range. A girl in a long white flowing gown astride a white stallion rode like the wind, her long black hair streaming behind her as she raced past him. A herd of wild horses followed close behind. Armin's heartbeat quickened, as he thought it to be Lilian. Again, the earth rumbled beneath him. A riding instructor followed by guests from the Pez Espada passed by on the ridge above him. Armin recognized one of the riders to be Giovanna's father. Relieved to know that he was in reality, he wiped his brow and then waved to the others as they disappeared out of sight.

He turned back to his ocean view in time to see a flock of seagulls now riding gracefully on a ribbon-like air current gliding freely out over the sea. Relaxing in the *now* he breathed in all of life. Again, the muffled sounds of a horse racing nearby startled him. Turning, he looked behind him; there, he saw Giovanna upon her white stallion galloping toward him. She slowed the horse by gently pulling up on the reins until the regal beast came to a stop. Easily, with a wide, graceful swing of her leg, she dismounted. It was obvious to him that she was a seasoned rider. "Got a minute?" Giovanna asked with a broad smile.

Armin answered without words. Spreading his arm wide, he guided her to where he sat on the cliff rock overlooking the sea. She seemed not to mind the rocky seat he offered. Armin noticed a vibrato quiver in her voice and body language that spoke of discomfort. He said nothing. He only sat back attentively listening to each word she spoke, as she shared her secrets with him. Armin motioned the other archers to begin without him, as he knew Giovanna's need to speak from her heart was more important for the time. For how often would she feel comfortable enough to pour her heart out to another she barely knew?

In a quiet voice, Giovanna told him of her mother's demise and of her gentleness, of all they shared together over the years, especially the secrets of their close relationship. It had only been the two of them for as long as she could remember. She missed her mother, and the anguish of her loss was growing. Confiding in Armin, she told of her father's long, hard hours at work and of how he was never there for either of them. "My father's behavior was odd and worsened as my mother's disease progressed." Blushing, she told him too of her father's improprieties with other women. Hatred and fear took its place on her face. "This was the reason for my mother's stress," she said. "She always worried about him and his indiscretions. My mother was a broken woman, and with this came disease finally bringing her to death. Now, my father, in his guilt, is overbearing. He is on top of my every move, involving himself in my decisions and in my life. He forgets somehow that I am not a child anymore. I try to forget the pain he brought us, but it is too late now for mending old wounds and I feel great resentment toward him. I do blame him for my mother's death." Her eyes welled with tears. She struggled to maintain composure. "If I could, I would leave him, never to see him again. My father acted as though he had done nothing wrong, playing both of us for fools. In the end, he is the fool; we knew all of what he had done, so foolish he was to insult us in this way. I weep for my mother."

Armin listened without speaking. Together, they sat on the rocks overlooking the sea listening to the waves hitting on the rocky shore below. He gently instructed her, "Breathe in, and breathe out . . . Again, take in a long, deep breath, hold it for a moment, and then release it. Good. Continue silently feeling the cadence of your own breath cycle . . . Good . . . Breathe in, and then let it go.

Exhale . . . Yes, keep breathing. Calm yourself—no tears, just breathe. There can be no ego, so let it go. Relax and fade into nothingness, and then stay on that plane for a while. Keep breathing. It is the cycle of all life. It is then you will hear the voice within you, knowing the truth of who you are." For a long time, there was silence. Armin then turned toward her. Staring into her blue eyes, which swelled red with tears, he took her hand in his and then spoke with an even tone. "Your father did not do anything to you or your mother; he did this to himself. You can only find the truth by letting your ego go. In silence, you will find your soul and the truth."

"It is only in still water that we can see."

—Taoist Proverb

"Giovanna, it will do you no good to hold resentment toward your father. He is only a man, who has made many mistakes. Yes! Now he tries to say he's sorry in his way. You may walk away from him with a heavy heart, stirring up painful and even ugly feelings now and again, or you can do the right thing and that is to forgive him once and let it go forever. Free yourself! Learn to communicate so that he knows your heart. Then let it be. Focus not on the past, for none of that can ever be changed or lived again. Meditate, find your center, still your mind, and calm your body. In this place, you will have knowledge and intuition. Be still, and listen—just listen. Accept what was, and live now in the moment you have before you. Find peace inside, and you will finally find love and harmony in your life. It will be a task of time, as what you hold on to will not easily be released. Focus on yourself; it is the only control you truly have. Dig deep, and realize who you are. For in the seeking of truth, you will find the root of yourself."

> Express yourself completely,
> Then keep quiet.
> Be like the forces of nature:
> When it blows, there is only wind:
> When it rains, there is only rain:
> When the clouds pass, the sun shines through,
> If you open yourself to the Tao,
> You are at one with the Tao
> And you can embody it completely.
> If you open yourself to insight,
> Then you are at one with insight
> And you can use it completely.
> If you open yourself to loss,
> Then you are at one with loss
> And you can accept it completely.
> Open yourself to the Tao,
> Then trust your natural responses
> And everything will fall into place.
>
> —Toa Te Ching
> Lao Tzu

By early afternoon, Giovanna had taken her place on the range. She lifted the bow and then eased it down in front of her chest as she took aim on the target. Armin watched, pleased in the knowledge, that she remembered her lessons with him.

The sun hung low in the sky, and a cool breeze swept in from the ocean. Together, Giovanna and her teacher walked back toward the targets, which sat on edge of the long stretch of beach leading up to the hotel. There stood her father watching from his place on the terrace. Somehow, Roberto knew that his daughter had confided in the Archer the secrets of her heart. Armin smiled as he delivered her to his hand. Tears streamed from Giovanna's eyes as she looked up to meet her father's gaze. Turning, she hugged Armin, holding him tight. Then, she looked at her father and led him back to the rocky ledge, which seemed to hold a bit of magic. From a distance, Armin watched for a time until he finally witnessed their embrace; he simply turned back toward the shop to lock up for the day. Swinging the sign on the door to read "closed," he sighed and then headed back to the quiet of his island hideaway on the hillside that overlooked the serenity of the sea.

# Chapter Eighteen
## His Truth Be Known

Armin showered, washing from his body salt left behind by the mist from the crashing waves at his favorite spot on the rocky ledge. Easing into nothingness, he let the warm, pulsating water melt every muscle in his body. He then stepped from the shower and wrapped a towel around his waist before walking outside with a cup of tea. Sitting in the small garden only steps from his door, Armin watched the wildlife and simple flight of a bumblebee drinking nectar from a nearby flower. Nature had found him, flooding him with gratitude. Preparing for his nightly ritual, he dressed in loose clothing and began his Taijiquan movements of grace that have no beginning and no end. He gathered chi in the same way each day. Slowly, the sky turned gray, darkening with the coming of night. Not yet was he willing to surrender to the abyss of sleep. He reached for his guitar, which stood just inside the doorway of the hut, and began playing and humming melodies he had stored in his head. It was the perfect end to his busy day.

The winds picked up, as if on cue, and the patter of rain began tapping on the canopy of palms overhead. Quickly, he grabbed his things and chose that night to sleep on a small couch inside the hut. Listening for a time to the changing rhythm of the rain as it pelted the roof and grounds surrounding him, Armin eventually floated away somewhere beyond this place. A voice spoke softly from the mist.

"There were troubles over land. The government took our properties, pitting neighbor against neighbor. My own family was in disbelief and could not understand why your father abandoned all he knew to become a warrior, solicited by lords, who controlled the land and farming industry." Armin began thrashing, kicking the back of the couch. Words screamed loudly in his subconscious as Lilian's voice grew louder, "You, Qin, were groomed to fight as your father. You were a great warrior, given a white stallion, who rode as fast as the wind. I watched you stalk across the fields in practice, listening to the thunder rumble the ground beneath you. I heard the clanking of the swords as your father prepared you for what was to come. My heart was broken and my spirit dying without you. I was young and immature, knowing nothing of the ways of men or life."

Armin tried to sit upright, hoping to wake up enough to find his voice, but no words would come. He watched as Lilian's flowing silk gown began to fade from sight. The Archer took a deep breath and blurted out, "I do remember you and knew that you would hold the answers to my dreams." Lilian materialized again, floating near him. Struggling to find his upright position, Armin grabbed the side of the old couch, letting his feet touch the gritty floor to steady himself. His eyes looked upon Lilian, who stood before him. She reached out to touch his skin feeling his warmth beneath her fingertips. Closing his eyes, he felt her touch and remembered fleeting scenes from centuries before. Without warning, his mind suddenly took a turn, traveling back to his last day in Beirut, the specific day he was visited by a man astride a white stallion, one who held a falcon on his sleeve. He finally recognized himself as the man in his vision. In a moment, his memory too turned to dust. Armin looked up high above the trees to see if Silverhawk was still resting in the palm. He was! The great bird stared at the Archer, directly letting him know his thoughts. "All is true, I have been with you since the beginning of each of your lives," a voice said. "I will be the one who will take you home in the end."

Silverhawk then spread his wings, lifted himself off his palm perch, and flapped wildly as he ascended into the darkness, leaving behind only the sounds of his wings beating a perfect cadence for his escape. Turning back, he saw that Lilian too was gone; leaving him to sit alone in the night remembering all that had been lost to him.

Morning had come with the fresh smell of fragrant flowers and wet scents from an earth cleansed by a fallen rain. His couch was not nearly as comfortable as his outside hammock but sufficed during occasional storms. Finding his way to the sink, Armin feverishly splashed cool water on his face, trying to erase any remnant of his dreams. He decided that a long walk in the coolness of the early morning would help to loosen his body. Along the many paths he followed, came flashes of himself upon his stallion. He lifted his arm high as if to hold a sword and then swung with a powerful downward motion, leveling the bushes that lined his path. There, before him, were the faces of many he had helped and also those he had fought. Thoughts came tearing into his mind, and for a moment, guilt ripped through him as he realized the pain he had brought to so many. He understood that it was then as it was now in this life, a trait he carried with him into the present. "The Bow Whisperer," as he was called, chose to live his life according to his own standards and beliefs and by his own decisions, certainly never to be told by others which path his life should take. A half smile crossed his face as he remembered his school days in Regensburg when even then he would never let another influence his way.

By all accounts, Armin was a soft-spoken, gentle man, yet inside of him was a sheath of steel to the core. He was steadfast in his convictions, and in this, he could not be swayed by anyone, even the likes of Lilian, the one who touched his heart. "Is this a trait of all archers?" he asked. "Or do I stand alone?" These traits were a part of him, ingrained as deeply as the firm sands that lined shores around the world. Never to be changed! He took these principles and beliefs, applying them to all he did—most important, in his teaching and shooting of the bow, he maintained total focus, breathing, empty-mindedness, and intention. With these, his arrow would find a target with precision and his life as well.

It was only after much thought along his walk that Armin put his ego aside, knowing now his father's grief, in losing his only son. Armin was disobedient to the wishes of his father to follow in his footsteps. He knew his heart well and which path would best satisfy the person he was then and now. The Bow Whisperer, Qin in that time, had no choice but to live in hiding, banished. He lived in solitude. Turning his face to the heavens, Armin screamed silently through his pain, realizing he had lost forever the woman and family he had loved at such a young age. He wondered if his current existence was his purgatory or hell. But why was this happening? Was the pain of recall too difficult to face? Or did he see in himself a softer side, one of caring in a human way. His many years of study and discipline brought him to a higher level of consciousness, a place out of the realm of most men. He was misunderstood by most who thought him to be cold and disconnected, when in fact; it was those who judged him who had no connection at all. Armin was anguished and challenged God to answer him. Then, he burst into tears, bowing his head as if in defeat. His father's words rang out to him as he remembered him, saying, "Now in death, I can see and respect the choices you made, my son. Although a boy in those times, you were more of a man than your own father." Rushing thoughts flashed again as he wondered about the life he was now living. A teacher and guide, he wandered through life alone. Briefly, Armin wondered if he had made the right decisions in this lifetime, but he quickly dismissed the notion. He was comfortable in his own skin, feeling a sense of freedom in his aloneness. This was his truth.

Armin was connected to China on a very profound level in his current life; it was there that he had found his true source of being. He had studied with masters the forms of Taijiquan. He learned of the Tao, disciplining himself in all things, knowing the way of the sword and of the bow and arrow. He was one with nature and in turn with the entire universe.

Armin spoke of being love itself, knowing his place of importance in the scheme of living. He was filled with inner peace, permitting all to flow naturally. Finally, exhaustion overtook him, and his mind could not think further of the past and circumstances that brought him to this place of contemplation.

Continuing on his walk, he left all thoughts behind, but not before offering a prayer to his father asking forgiveness for the pain and dishonor he brought to all his family in a time long past, saying in a hushed voice, "I had loved and missed you, Father; forgive me. I was young and bullheaded then, filled with the strength of youth and foolishness of my ego mind." He lifted his head to the sky, happy to see the new dawn was now bright with sun. His walk was over, and his mind was at ease. Weary from a thought-filled morning, he rested in the garden near his door. In stillness, he sat, empty-minded in a void where nothing could reach him. Awakening from his rest, he was refreshed as if a weight had been lifted from him.

# Chapter Nineteen

# Closure

*A*rmin had been summoned to the city by Fernando Maas, director of tourism, who wanted to discuss with him the possibility of bringing archery to many other hotels on the island of Mallorca. Together, the Archer and Maas mingled their ideas as they discussed locations, budgets, equipment, and the staff needed to succeed in this new venture. At the conclusion of their meeting, both were pleased with the progress they had made; they shook hands, agreeing to meet the following week with the entire council of tourism, bringing to them an equitable proposal. Stepping out into the busy street, Armin was rushed by people tending to the busyness of their day. Hunger gnawed at him, and he found a small café where he ate a hardy lunch and sipped on his usual mocha, as he watched life passing before him, shaking his head at the bedlam he saw. Armin felt very comfortable with his choice to live in a simple, uncomplicated way, void of the confusion brought on by modern conveniences and the social media of the times. While having his lunch, he thought about teaching new archers and those who would work behind the scenes running each new business. He was certain all would be in accordance with his ideas and philosophy of the bow. Once established, his new staff would handle the business during Armin's absence. He spent the remainder of the afternoon walking the city, admiring the ancient and modern architectural influences and reminding himself of his own designs and the creations he once dreamed of building. The day was his to do with what he chose. Refreshed to be away from his routine, he kept walking the small alleyways off the main streets. Small shops filled with treasures and bakeries sent their candied scents into the air, reminding him of his childhood days of exploration in Regensburg. With late afternoon approaching, Armin left the confusion of the town behind, finding a path to the ocean where he would watch the sun bow to the darkness of the sky, ending another day. With the last bit of light fading below the horizon, Armin found his way up the long, dusty road leading to his private world overlooking the sea.

Stillness filled the night air and was broken only by the sounds of a hoot owl and an occasional croaking of tree frogs. He did not sense the nearness of visitors from the past and was relieved that sleep would carry him into the next day.

In a short time, prancing hooves danced around his bed, startling him. "Wake, my son!" the voice commanded. With this, Silverhawk's great wings flapped wildly and his screams pierced the night. Armin sat upright, prepared to face his ancient father once more. Looking into his eyes, he recognized a familiar expression on the face of the old man. It was gentle, and his calm eyes conveyed his desire for peace and acceptance, but even more apparent was his need for the love of his only son. The ancient warrior spoke about their family and of the pain Qin had left in the wake of his disappearance. Sorrowfully, his father asked, "Whatever had become of you?"

Compassionately, Armin tried to explain his reasons for leaving. "Father," he said, "the decision to leave my family and Lilian behind did not come with ease. I was a hunted man then because I chose not to fight for the dynasty. I found refuge in the mountains. There, I was seeking the wisdom of the elders and monks who lived in seclusion with their own among the forests and streams of the mythical mountain. I did this, so I could learn their way of accepting life as it is without expectations, validating the truth in the depth of my convictions. Never did I mean to banish myself from those I loved, but as time passed, I changed, knowing myself and my purpose. For how can any man be good for another if he is not good for himself? When I left my home and family, I made a firm decision. If I will fight, it will be for the lesser force. I fight for the one who is frail against the roar of the lion. My sword is mighty and fierce when raised. I have learned that it is better never to fight another man's battle. I was not a coward or one to run away, yet I was left no choice in this. I could never harm our own people for another's cause. I now make these same decisions in this new life. Look," he said, spreading his arms wide. "My life is now filled with beauty all around me. I have learned to look only at the moment in front of me and to relish the life within it. If I do not do this, then I will have missed the precious moment given me. This, Father, is the true way of a warrior, not to fight as in battle or to raise arms against another. The warrior is peaceful, taking action with no action. He says little, and in this, he is as loud as the roar of a tiger leaving his opponent to fight only with his ego. The true warrior lives a simple life of humility, moderation, and compassion. Do you not remember the teachings of the Tao? I understand your desire is for me to return to my roots, the place of my ancient beginning, and to be with you again. Perhaps one day I will, but for now, I still have much work to do here." The two nodded as if in understanding, and the vision disappeared as quickly as it had arrived. Armin fell into the arms of sleep as peace took its place within, bringing him to a new dawn.

# Chapter Twenty

# Later Years in Europe

*T*ime passed on the island of Mallorca. Never again after his ancient father's last visit did Armin see either him or Lilian. His life was guided purely by the need to share his story of the bow with those he taught—to give his wisdom to those who would listen. Armin developed a heart-to-heart connection with each student, as every one of them had a tale to tell, a story hidden deep inside. The Archer's sensitivity and knowledge of such things brought to each of them a silent closeness for he could see into their souls. As with Zu-Ling and Fredric, he could soften their hearts by simply showing them another way.

Armin worked with boundless passion, creating manuals of verbal and pictorial drawings, intertwining the two as one, so others would better understand his method of instinctive shooting. Word spread of his teaching and the novel archery techniques he implemented, drawing individuals from around the globe, seeking to train with him using these new skills. Luckily, the development of his new businesses with the help of Fernando Maas proved to be highly successful, bringing more tourists and financial stability to the island.

An early Sunday morning brought him a surprising desire to read the newspaper. Armin gathered a few things and walked down the hillside to the local drugstore to make his purchase. There was no sun in the sky, and a cloudy mist filled the morning air; he found his way to the bench outside the archery shop and sat listening to the waves as he thumbed through the paper. An article in the sports section drew his attention. It was about students whom he had taught from around the globe. He smiled and was enthusiastic to complete the words in front of him. It told of an archery competition that had taken place in the south of Germany a week earlier. Armin knew of these competitions as he himself had participated in them in times long past. John Garner, a sports journalist covering the story, was astonished to witness four archers who shot only with glistening arrows that appeared to be made of gold. The article went on to tell of their expertise in handling the bow and how they hit the target dead-on with each shot. The sportswriter interviewed each of them, and all told the same story of the Archer, Armin Hirmer, of his way and philosophy in using the bow. Each story was detailed, and Armin took his newspaper inside where reflections would not obscure the words he read. Finishing the article, Armin was thrilled with his former students' accomplishments; he was pleased to know they had found one another after all these years. He hoped the messages left for them inscribed on each arrow had found a place in their souls, changing them forever.

Armin's hair had grayed with the passing of time. His body, still strong, longed again for another adventure to stir his soul, another place for his eyes to see. Never planning too far into the distance, he always made his decisions a short time before his departure. With the first inkling to move forward in his life, Armin gathered his belongings from his mountain retreat, readying to leave this place he loved. Two days had passed, and he felt safe with his decision to walk forward in his life leaving behind all he had worked for. He carried one suitcase along with a neatly packed long sleeve containing his bow. In another case, his arrows were packed securely for their next journey. Keeping his decision to leave private, Armin told only a few staff members. They knew his way and never would interfere or dare ask the reasons for his coming and going. Their only hope was that he would find his way back to them in time to come.

Only a brief moment of sadness filled Armin, as it did with each departure. He would miss the beauty of Mallorca, his mountain hideaway that overlooked the vastness of a turquoise sea, and the many friends he had made—especially Nita, for she was the one who always stood by ready to assist in any way she could. He would leave a small piece of himself behind knowing that time would not permit his return. On his way to the airport, he stared out the window of the cab capturing the island scenes and embedding them forever in his memory. Upon his arrival, he saw many friends he knew and others who had taken lessons from him. Shaking hands, they joked briefly and said their good-byes. He made certain that his belongings were safe and secure, watching with a careful eye as his precious cargo was loaded onto the plane. Once aboard, he found his way to a window seat. Relaxing in the moment, he let his feelings leave him and thought little of the path to come, trusting God's hand would guide him.

The journey would be long from Mallorca. Armin would first fly to Munich for a change of planes and then on to the Great Republic of China, landing in Peking. Peering from the window of the plane, he felt excitement as he moved forward into a new adventure.

The plane climbed, finding its way into high altitudes. Soaring above the clouds, his mind wandered back to the island of Mallorca where he had stayed for many more years than any other place he had visited. He wondered if any of his former students would look for him there, as he had not said good-bye to any of them in a proper way. These thoughts would reoccur and then flee as he turned his attention to reading and working on his newest manual.

Soon enough, the pilot announced their estimated time of arrival in Munich. A feeling of exhilaration flowed through him as the first leg of his journey would soon be over. The next day, he found himself on yet another tarmac waiting for takeoff, this time to his final destination, China. Buckled into a gray and red leather seat, Armin looked out at the tarmac from Air China's jet. His thoughts drifted to all the many places he had been—Beirut, Gran Canary, Mallorca, Sylt, Austria, and Malta—and to the many cities and seaports in Europe that he had touched with his teaching. The unknown brought Armin a sense of exhilaration, and he looked forward to whatever awaited him in the mountains of Wudang.

Once in Peking, Armin taxied into the city and found a modest hotel for the night. Placing his belongings safely in his room, he walked the streets taking in the scenery as he looked for a restaurant in which to satisfy his hunger. The flashing lights decorated the buildings of the city and smells of food filled the evening air bringing back many memories of when he had visited so long ago. That first night, he rested well and was ready at the crack of dawn to continue his journey to the mountains. After purchasing his tickets, Armin boarded the soft sleeper train, which would take him another twenty hours to Wudang Shan.

A year after his departure from Mallorca, one student did return seeking to find the Archer. Giovanna wanted to thank him for helping her unravel the mysteries that had troubled her youth. Armin helped mend the wounds she carried from her mother's death and repair her relationship with her father. Twelve years had passed since her first visit to Mallorca, and she was now busy with her own family. She always remembered Armin fondly.

Giovanna and her family had arrived at the Pez Espada. Settling into their room, they rested for a short time. With her husband and children in tow, she explored all the new amenities and changes made to the hotel since her visit years earlier. Looking to the target area, she scanned the grounds, hoping to find Armin. She was drawn back toward the sea and the rocky ledge where they had spent hours repairing her inner turmoil. In silence, she reminisced. Armin was the only one who could reach her, giving her a new perspective on life. Remembering him with gratitude, she felt uplifted, as though a robe of lead weights had been taken from her shoulders. She glowed then with newness and an enlightened spirit carrying the same feelings into the present.

Their family vacation to Mallorca was her choice. She felt it time to introduce Luciano, Enzo, and Gina to the man she credited with changing her. Her children were now old enough to study with her favorite teacher, and the thought of it brought her great pleasure. One last time, she looked near the range for the Archer and then followed the path to the small archery shop only to find a note left on the door simply stating *"Closed."* Seeing Fernando, another of the archers who had worked with Armin, Giovanna inquired of Armin's whereabouts. Fernando thought she looked familiar, yet he was unable to remember her specifically. There were so many guests who had come and gone through the years. He simply wasn't sure. Fernando recognized the urgency in her voice and then told her of Armin's departure from the island the year before.

Saddened, she felt a sense of great loss. Turning from him, she and her children wandered out toward the rocky ledge where she and Armin had spent time speaking of life's lessons. As they threw rocks out into the crashing surf below, she told Enzo and Gina about the archer and her lessons with him, lessons he had taught her from this very same ledge twelve years earlier. Silently, she wondered why he had never mentioned his leaving in the few emails they shared through the years.

Giovanna; her husband, Luciano; and their children enjoyed the resort's pools, horseback riding, and the nightly evening musical entertainment. In the days to follow, Giovanna thought nothing was the same without Armin, and she was angry with herself that she had not spoken from her heart, thanking him and showing her appreciation all those years ago. Several days later, Fernando approached her at the pool asking to speak to her alone. She excused herself, leaving her husband's side to see what was so important. They walked out onto the range area, which was empty at the noon hour. From his quiver, Fernando pulled a golden arrow, light weight and glowing as if brand-new. Giovanna looked at him inquisitively not understanding what this was. He told her that the arrow had been left for her by the Archer. She looked at him confused, and he continued, "This was a gift left behind especially for you. Your teacher asked me to make sure I delivered it in person, if ever you were to return. In my dream last night, I saw you with the Archer out on the rocky ledge. I then remembered who you were." Giovanna was surprised and honored that Armin would remember her out of all the students he had worked with. Examining every inch of the arrow, she discovered an inscription beneath its feathers. After reading the engraved message, she stretched her arm out toward Fernando, showing him what was written. Tears streamed down her face as she grabbed his hand, thanking him. She was certain that the Archer had left this message only for her. Looking into the young man's eyes, she said, "How is it that he knew me so well? Look." Fernando knew the message but looked again to appease Giovanna. "'Be silent, and hear your soul speak to you. Do not judge, instead find love and give it in return.' Because of the Archer, I chose a career working with orphans and abused children. I learned to give them a second chance."

# Chapter Twenty-One

## Mirrored Images

*A*rmin's return to Wudang Shan gave him a feeling of excitement, which stirred memories from times of long ago. In this sacred place, he found comfort in his life, unlike anywhere else in the world, bringing him peace and tranquility. The mountains were remote, losing themselves in lush forests riddled with streams, caves, and all the best nature had to offer. Paradise, as he knew it, was far from the cities and the commotion of civilization. As he traveled to his destination, Armin noticed the many changes that had taken place since his visit as a younger man. Even the landscapes had changed, bringing a new era marked with modern technology. New buildings sat on every corner in the lower cities. Reminiscing, he looked from the bus as he ascended the majestic mountain, witnessing views of endless skies and clouds floating below him. Here, Armin would reconnect to his source, which remained firmly rooted inside of him. Haunting dreams of his ancient past now began to enter his mind. He believed that his warrior father would finally rest in peace, knowing his son inevitably chose to return home.

With a group of others, Armin traveled by bus from the city of Shiyan. The long, winding road to the Golden Cloud Temple allowed him to reunite with his past. Upon arrival at their destination, the guests filed off the overcrowded bus. Welcoming guides eagerly waited to assist the new arrivals with their luggage and to direct them to their sleeping quarters. A middle-aged monk looked at Armin questioningly and then put his hand out to assist with his gear. Gladly, Armin handed the stranger his one suitcase. They bowed to one another in respect, and then turning, they walked the roadway leading to a small house where Armin would stay the night. His room was simple; it had two single beds, one at each end of the room. There was a colorful wooden screen, which offered privacy. A small dresser stood against the back wall while a square table and two chairs sat in the middle of the room. A large colorful vase of fragrant flowers stood atop the table, filling the room with sweet aromas and welcoming him.

Speaking in broken English, the monk asked Armin if he would like to eat. Armin appreciated the offer but preferred to rest after his long journey. They bowed once again, and the monk went on his way. Lying on one of the beds, Armin took a late-afternoon nap, which took him well into the early evening hours. When he awoke, he stretched his weary body with easy movements of Taijiquan. A sudden knock on the door startled him. Opening the red-painted wooden door, Armin was surprised to see his guide standing there with a broad smile and several bags of food in one hand. In the other hand, he held a pot of brewed tea. Armin welcomed the monk into his small room, thanking him for his thoughtful gesture. They sat at the small table where they shared dinner and spoke of many things. Armin noticed the monk looking at him in a peculiar way. Without warning, the monk reached over and touched the top of Armin's head as if to feel the texture of his graying hair. Thinking this was odd, Armin looked at him, trying to find a hint of familiarity that would explain his behavior. The monk reached over the table and felt Armin's face. This man in monk's clothing closed his eyes as if he were blind. With his fingers, he traced each furrow of Armin's face. Knowing this was not of tradition; Armin sensed gentleness, as if this young monk's hand felt things from his heart, things unseen that only came from the sensitivity of knowing. So he permitted the touching. Without warning, the monk's eyes began to flow with tears as he recognized the one who sat before him. "You are 'the Archer.' Others have called you, 'the Bow Whisperer.' You are the one who travels with your spirit guide Silverhawk."

"Yes," the Archer replied.

Speculatively, Armin looked at the monk's face, which had changed color. Unable to contain himself further, he blurted out his name, "I am Bolin." With this, from beneath his dark blue robes, he pulled a golden arrow. Handing it to the Archer, he said, "You left this for me in the field of my father's land many, many years ago. It was because of the message on the arrow that I chose to become a monk. I realized that the discipline of the bow that you taught and the lessons of the Tao were intertwined."

Armin looked beneath the feathers, and there, it said, *"When you find the greatest of the three treasures of the Tao, compassion, you will have found your Way."*

Bolin then explained, "One must find one's way to compassion first by understanding all of the Tao in order to find the truth."

Elated, the men embraced, filling the small room with a true sense of homecoming. Long into the night, the two spoke of Bolin's father, Hai, and of his mother, Lihua, discussing details of their passing. From the sadness of death to the magic of life, Bolin shared with delight the story of Meifeng's marriage and the birth of her son. Armin was happy to hear such news. Bolin spoke with delight of his sixteen-year-old nephew, an archer, taught by his parents in the same way Armin had taught them. Obviously, youth and time had not distorted Bolin's memory of the past. After dinner was over and the conversation complete, the two men stood facing one another; without words, they began the movements of Taijiquan. Mirroring their images, they found solace sharing the flow of grace and beauty, much like the synchronized flowing of a river weaving its way to nowhere. Both men were grounded into the earth and centered to its core like a rock, just as they had been at the small house in the woods so long ago. Armin fondly recalled the morning he felt eyes upon his back, only to turn and see young Bolin and Meifeng mimicking his flowing movements. The delightful sounds of youthful innocence and the giggling of two children so very long ago still rang in the Archer's ears as he remembered his time with Hai, Lihua, and the children. After much time, their bodies fell silent; darkness had crept in with the setting of the sun, and their eyes were heavy. A good night's sleep would give them an advantage for their next day's journey to the summit above the Golden Temple.

## Pales of Night

Armin offered Bolin the spare bed, which was hidden behind the carved wooden screen. Accepting the offer, Bolin fell swiftly into the arms of sleep. The monk's small, snorting noises kept Armin awake well into the night. Not used to sharing a room with another, he preferred the symphony of nature to which he was accustomed. In time, Armin drifted to a quiet place deep inside of himself. Dreams began to swirl in his head, and his subconscious drew images of the past. The cries of Silverhawk and the sound of beating wings filled Armin's head, warning of visions to come. Visualizing a speck of darkness in the skies below the mountain, he watched as Silverhawk glided freely toward him making his way home. Happy with the return of his spirit guide, Armin drifted more deeply into the void of nothingness.

*Taking Armin by surprise, Lilian chose to reveal herself once more after nearly sixteen years. At first, she sat at the edge of his bed just watching him as she always had. Music played softly somewhere in the distance. Her slender white fingers softly touched his face, as warmth raced through her delicate body. Armin looked upon Lilian, whispering of her beauty beneath his breath. He had longed for her return through the years, wondering why she had never come back to him. Now, his desire for her was overwhelming; he found himself easily aroused. Staring into her eyes, he allowed her to look into the window of his soul. Never before had he permitted anyone to look at him in this way.*

*Lifting his arm, he reached for her and in a gentle motion, drew her to him. Armin pulled Lilian so close he could smell the sweetness of her skin. One look from her pierced his heart, and in turn, his heart pounded wildly and his loins throbbed. He needed to feel all of her. As he held her face in his hands, Armin's lips found her mouth supple and wet, tasting of ginger. Her breath was sweet and awakened sensations that had been lost to him. Feeling her soft, warm skin against him, he wrapped his arms tightly around her waist. He savored the moment, knowing it might never be again. Closing his eyes, he laid her beside him and slowly ran his fingers down her spine following the graceful arches of her back. Rhythmic movements of their naked bodies solidified their wanting. Lilian forcefully pushed her body deep into him, never wanting their union to end. Armin could not take his eyes away from her face. Lilian's gentle groaning excited him even more, and through the night, he watched her eyes explode with passion as she reached the pinnacle of ecstasy many times, melting them into one. Lost in the pales of the night which sailed far beyond the universe their joy ended abruptly as quickened heartbeats exploded into nothingness.*

The sun's ray beamed through the window, blinding Armin and waking him from his elusive dream. Morning had come too swiftly; he could not move, wanting to stay lost in his thoughts of Lilian. Slowly, Armin opened his eyes to find his arms encircled, holding on to nothing but empty air. He dared not think the image in his dreams was a fantasy. Reaching his arms out for Lilian, he discovered she was gone. Armin then listened for Bolin wondering if he was aware of his night visitor. Sighing, he was relieved to discover the room was empty. Armin dressed quickly to answer a knock on the door of his room. Bolin stood before him with a broad smile on his face, baring all his teeth. In his hands, he carried a tray with tea and a variety of fruits for the offering of a simple breakfast. Armin invited the monk inside, pleased to see the food, for he was famished. Grateful for their reaquaintence, they sat in silence thankful for all the blessings before them. As they ate, Armin's mind took him far from reality off to a plane beyond where they sat. He could not help himself as thoughts of Lilian kept coming back. She had awakened all his senses.

When the two men had finished breakfast, they packed a few belongings and stepped outside. Looking outward, they appreciated the beauty of the sunlit day. Variegated hues of greens and purple filled their earthly scene. Above and below were wisps of white clouds floating on a pale-blue sky. They breathed deeply, as if the breath itself was food for their souls. And it was. In awe of the view, neither spoke, for the whispers of the trees and the stillness of this place were enough.

In the distance, Armin recognized the shrill cry of Silverhawk. Looking down the mountainside, he watched as the great bird glided toward him. Thumping sounds of the bird's great wings were echoed on the steady breeze as he approached. Silverhawk's wings made a sound like that of a motored fan as they were sent into slow motion, backstroking as thousands of feathers halted the force of his flight. Armin extended his arm high in the air. Silverhawk landed on his old friend, as he had so many times in the distant past. Armin felt a chill run through his body, confirming his return to these sacred mountains was in alignment with his soul.

"Wudang Shan's South Cliff—Tianyi Stone Temple"—
"Cherry Collins, www.SurreyandHantsTaiChi.com"

## The Summit

Gonging temple bells rang throughout the valley floor as birds sang their early praises to the dawning of a new day and the chirps of crickets filled the woodlands. Their songs rising on the morning mist hung high over the canopied forest. Armin was happy to be home in this place he loved and easily became lost in its beauty. The two men walked the steep path to the summit of the Golden Temple, and bright sun warmed their faces as a light breeze cut the sting of its rays. Reaching their destination by midafternoon, Bolin spread his arms wide as he gestured to Armin to take in the vista. Armin fell silent, walking to the edge of the mountain. Lost in thought, he was amazed and humbled by the wonders looking back at him. This was the home of Taoism, where during meditation, the connection between one's mind, body, and spirit aligned with ease in the presence of the Source. Bolin called to Armin, disrupting his concentration. He directed his attention to the old tree, the same one he had fallen against in the raging storm years earlier, the same tree that bore the golden arrow. Leaning against it, he smelled its sweet wood, which triggered memories of that perilous day. Turning to view the vast scene before him, he noticed a lone building, painted red and standing against the backdrop of blue skies. Bewildered, Armin looked toward Bolin for an explanation of the house, yet he was nowhere to be found. Armin called out his name, and Bolin then appeared from the small building that clung to the windy mountain. In his hand, he carried a bow and a quiver, revealing the glow of one golden arrow. A flush ran through Armin as he reached for his old quiver, recognizing the arrow of gold protected by its leather sheath. Armin searched the shaft and found a worn engraved message beneath its feathers. These were his belongings lost to the storm that had swept across the mountain so many years before. Draped across Bolin's arm were flowing garments of black silk, with sashes of braided leather. In the other hand, he carried riding boots and leather chaps. Reaching out his arm to Armin, he said, "These too are yours."

Questioningly, Armin searched Bolin's face for the answer. Finally, he asked, "What are these garments? They do not belong to me."

Bolin responded, "These are the same garments worn by warriors in ancient times. It would please many for you to have them now."

Bolin went on, "Your story has been told throughout the mountains for over thirty years. The elder monks and masters who were here at the time you studied saw in you a special man, one who used his sword and the way of the bow in harmony. They said that your heart was pure; your intent was for the good of all men. The truth of living is in the teaching of the Tao. You understood this, giving devotion to these lessons in your own way. Many times, the elders spoke of your openness and the generosity of your teachings, knowing this would lead others to the truth of life. The monks in their wisdom knew in time that you would return." Bolin explained, "Five years after your parting, it was decided that this place be built in your honor to keep those things you had left behind. Today, I am privileged to be the one giving them back to you." Armin could not speak yet; his mind questioned how it was that Bolin knew of his ancient father. Then he realized there was no mystery in this at all. Bolin intuitively knew of Armin's life and the truth of his past. Glancing into each other's eyes, neither man wanted to look too deeply into the soul of the other—for eyes are the windows to man's innermost secrets, to his faults, regrets, and even the guilt that can follow him throughout his life.

Armin's time was precious to him, and he looked forward to being alone on the mountain. Bolin well understood his need and without words, the two men silently walked in different directions, leaving Armin behind to awaken to the universe.

As time passed, months turned into years of silence between the two; each understood the other. Bolin did not worry about his friend and his elusiveness, as he knew Armin's abilities to make everything out of nothing, trusting the universe for his safety.

# Chapter Twenty-Two

## Ten Years Later

*I*t was early spring in the tenth year after Armin's return to Wudang, and visitors from around the globe were again descending on this well-known paradise. Buses arrived on schedule, bringing with them tourists looking to find the magic these sacred mountains offered. Some were students on holiday. Others were there looking to check off one more box on their bucket list. The more serious came to learn of the miraculous healing power of meditation. Of martial arts, Taijiquan, qigong, archery, and the Dance of the Swords. One group on the bus that day had met years earlier at an archery competition in Germany. Their visit now to China was a testament to their teacher, who had invisibly bonded them together, solidifying their lives as one in common. The ride up the hillside was filled with stories from each of them telling of their bond and the influence that the Archer had had on them. Salina was shy in comparison to the others; her excitement somehow exploded as she told stories of her relationship with her coach and teacher. She spoke of her school days in Beirut and how she knew of his dreams in those times. "I have become an artist. I own a studio in the town of Baabda near the sea. There, I am able to place my thoughts on a canvas for all to enjoy. And it is only because of him that I use my talent in this way."

Sishiba then shared her own story. "I have continued in my studies, finding my gift of knowing to be helpful in my practice of psychology. I feel as though I have been able to continue the philosophy taught by the Archer. He said, 'Use your gifts for the good of others.' And I am."

Age was catching up with Bolin; his beard was now graying, and his back hunched as if his head were stuck in a downward position watching every step he took. This condition was from an injury he had sustained as a teenager, making it seem that his physical body preceded his years. Exercise and movements of Taijiquan kept his body agile, allowing him to walk with the grace of a tiger. Sitting on a bench near the square, Bolin watched for the buses from the lower valley, which arrived daily from the city of Shiyan. There were clanking sounds, and a noisy muffler roared and hissed, sending out black smoke from its tailpipe as the lone bus chugged along the sloppy road, tired of the trek it made. As the bus came to its final stop, Bolin felt compelled to assist the passengers in whatever way he could.

One by one, the visitors filed off the bus, and he bowed to each in greeting. One woman with long black hair, perhaps in her late thirties, struggled with her backpack; it had caught on another passenger's bag, ripping the back pocket. Many of its contents were sent flying all over the stairs leading off the bus. Embarrassed, the woman immediately bent down to assemble her belongings as she mumbled something foul under her breath. Noticing sandaled feet and flowing dark-blue fabric, she was startled to see the arms of a stranger reaching out to lend a hand. She lifted her red face to meet Bolin's eyes. Her heart raced and then sank, mortified that the monk may have heard her words. "I am sorry for this," she said as she urgently tried to repack what had fallen from her bag. "I thank you for your kindness." She nodded to him and was met with a warm smile.

Bolin noticed a golden hue on the fletching of an arrow, which stuck out from her backpack when she bent over. He knew right then her reason for coming to this place, and his smile broadened. Her friends traveling with her reached her side and also offered assistance. Bolin bowed, greeting each of them. The visitors respectfully bent at their waists to acknowledge this Chinese tradition, and three more golden arrows revealed themselves.

Turning, Bolin gestured for the new guests to follow him. Silently, the small group grabbed their bags and fell in line trying to keep pace with him, while other visitors waited for their guides to arrive. They walked for some time, and the monk listened to their conversations as he silently led the way through the crooked streets. Each turn in the road offered incredible scenes, bringing sighs and words of appreciation from the newcomers. Silence then took its place with all but one, who proclaimed tiredness and shortness of breath because of the high altitude. They passed several buildings and temples along the way. They were adorned with carved pillars featuring dragons.

Eventually, they approached a temple of gold with a curved roof and ancient carvings of birds and lotus flowers. Bolin motioned for them to sit on the steps outside as he climbed the long staircase and disappeared out of sight. Trusting the monk, they spoke of the Archer, anticipating their reunion with him as they waited for their guide to return.

Soon, Bolin appeared, bringing with him three other monks dressed in flowing brown robes. Two younger monks stood on either side of the one of great age, assisting him. The elder monk wore a garment of gold signifying his high status in Buddhism. "He is nearing one hundred years of age," Bolin whispered. The elder's eyes were mere slits, and deep lines seemingly carved into his leathered face brought character and dimension to his smile. The elder monk slowly approached them; leaning on a long, sleek staff. Gracefully, he bowed as low as he could. Reaching his long, slender hand into their backpacks, he pulled from them the golden arrows for his viewing. Looking each in the eye, he then turned and pointed beyond to the high mountain, home of the Archer.

Excitement poured from him as he spoke in Chinese to Bolin then with a nod of his head. He smiled and bowed. Without hesitation, he returned the arrows to their rightful owners and walked away, headed to the holy temple. Seeing confusion written on the faces of the five visitors, Bolin then said in English, "He is Xizang Da Cheng, a holy man, my teacher and master. I have studied with him since I was very young. He has great wisdom and has taught me well. Xizang Da Cheng knows the one you look for, for he too taught the same one you seek. We can see that you have also met the same warrior, who in his turn has taught you well. Coming to this place is a testament and honor to him."

The visitors looked up the stairs to see the old monk turn toward them once more. Raising his hands into a prayer position, he bowed before retreating inside the temple. They all found themselves mimicking the monk's gesture, honoring him in return.

Chatter between the five amplified. "How is it that they know who we look for?" Sishiba then spoke out. "We are here to find the Archer," she said as she pointed to her arrow and its message. Bolin simply waved his hand and walked toward the path to the mountain. Again, Sishiba insisted that Bolin communicate with her. Raising her voice, she repeated herself as she ran to him and stood in his face defiantly. "Please answer me, sir! We are here to see the Archer. You know him, don't you?"

Bolin simply looked beyond the woman and waved to the rest of them to follow. He led them through several narrow grassy pathways lined with brown, rocky dirt. The group followed Bolin to a long line of connected buildings, each with curved roofs and carvings adorning the intricate moldings. Bolin opened the gate to one of the homes that were stacked one next to the other, telling the group to walk ahead through the opened door.

They were greeted inside by an elderly woman dressed in baggy gray pants with a matching mandarin-collared shirt. She said with a thick Mandarin accent, "Come in; this is where you will rest for the night to get ready for your adventure tomorrow." The women giggled while the men let out an "Amen." Each of them looked about the small quarters while relishing the smells of cooked food coming from the kitchen. Soon, they were given bowls of rice and Chinese vegetables, and, at last, a round of perfectly brewed tea. A conversation stirred between them; curiosity was aroused within each. They were all asking why they could not get a straight answer from the monk concerning the whereabouts of the Archer. Patience was a virtue the Archer taught them. "All will come at the right time. Do not rush or become anxious, for it will do you no good. Trust in God, as his time is the right time for all things to happen," the Archer would say. Now, they were put to the test. Remembering his words, they waited for morning to arrive, hoping they would find the answers they were seeking.

The small group of guests awakened early, anticipating the day to follow when a tapping on the door interrupted their planning. There stood the same monk who had guided them to their sleeping quarters. He waved to them, saying, "Come with me." Immediately, Giovanna and Fredric went to the kitchen to thank the woman appropriately. Her name was Chenquang, meaning *morning light*. Not speaking Chinese well enough, they told her as best they could of the monk's arrival and thanked her for the breakfast she had served. Andrew and Sishiba gathered their belongings, excited to be on the move again. Outside, the monk bowed to them and finally introduced himself. "I am Bolin." In return, his movements were respectfully met with a nod of the head and a deep bow.

Bolin led them up the long, winding trail that wove itself in between gorges and mountains. Clearings offered views never before seen by these people who had come seeking their teacher. Camera lenses clicked, capturing what seemed to be surreal. Only the sounds of wildlife mixed with the stirring of the leaves blown by mountain winds could be heard.

Their voices dimmed in the mist that surrounded them. They were certain they were entering the gates of heaven. Their muscles were weakened by the climb, and breathlessness overtook a few, but the group was not deterred, knowing their prize awaited them atop the mountain. Looking ahead, they could see the monk had already reached the summit. Determined, they placed their feet on solid ground, pushing upward until they finally reached the end of their journey. Silence befell the captivating scene in front of them. There were no temple bells or calling of birds, only the sight of winged butterflies swarming the small bushes that spotted the earth at this gateway to the universe. They stood motionless, mesmerized by the magnificence before them.

Perhaps at that very moment, they knew what lived in the heart of the Archer more than at any other time. There was something magic in this place, for each of them had been touched as well. Breaking the silence, Sishiba and Fredric spoke at the same time, saying, "We have come to see the Archer. There is a bird that follows him, a spirit guide, known as Silverhawk."

"He has been called the 'Bow Whisperer,'" Giovanna interjected. "Have you heard of this name?" All eyes looked upon Bolin's face.

"The golden arrows directed us to this place of such majesty," Andrew said.

Taking the arrow in hand, Giovanna boldly showed the monk its shaft. "Look!" she said. "It reads 'Wudang, China' in very small print. We have all been guided to this place. Please help us!" she pleaded with tears welling in her eyes. The others took their arrows and put them in front of Bolin as well. He knew the heaviness of their hearts yet said nothing, which frustrated them even more. The group looked upon Bolin, each wondering if the monk before them spoke English well enough to tell them what they needed to know.

Bolin looked at them and told them to sit on the ground cross-legged as he was. "Be silent," he said. "Empty your heads. And do as he always told you. Let your mind create your world. Be still, listen to the wind, and feel its strength. It is then that you will know your truth, understanding the secrets of life."

*"When you lose all sense of self, the bonds of a thousand chains will vanish. Lose yourself completely. Return to the root of the root of your own soul."*

*(Rumi)*

Frustrated, they did as Bolin said; knowing in the end their quest to reunite with the Archer would come to fruition. Finding themselves engaged with the universe, they sank deep into a place they had not known before. They felt a reverence, an unexplainable consumption of their entire beings. As they sat on the earth, enfolded by clouds, they gazed at the opening to heaven. There, in the presence of God, they felt kindness and understanding walk into them; euphoria took them over. For some time, Bolin let them stay within themselves, allowing each to absorb the newest from the Source. The sound of footsteps broke their trance. Three others, coming from a small red building that clung to the mountain, joined them. They approached the group holding bows for each person who sat before them. A handsome man in his late forties introduced himself. "My name is Zu-Ling." Turning, he introduced the others. "This is my wife, Meifeng, and our son, Armin Zhanshi Choi." Without hesitation, Bolin then placed his hand beneath his flowing robe and pulled from it a golden arrow. A gasp came from the others, as they realized that he too had been touched by the teachings of the man they called the Archer.

"He knows him!" one shouted, and then they all stood planting their feet firmly on the earth. The others joined in, asking where the Archer was and why Bolin had not told them earlier.

Bolin simply replied, "All things have a time of happening."

Bolin then lifted his golden arrow, pointing the tip toward the circle of others and said, *"Compassion."*

Fredric followed, *"Forgiveness."*

The two looked toward Giovanna, who then held her arrow outward in the same way, saying, *"Understanding."*

Sishiba said, *"Awareness."*

And Salina said, *"Loving-kindness."*

Placing the tip of his arrow on the other five in the circle, Zu-Ling read the message, which had dulled with time. *"Diligence."* Zu-Ling then shared the Archer's wisdom, "Be pleased with all you are and all you do. In this, there is great joy. *You have nothing to prove to anyone other than yourself.* Be patient."

"Where is he?" the group exclaimed.

Bolin then spread his arms wide like a great bird stretching its wings. "He is here." Bolin reached his arms out toward the universe, turning 360 degrees. Gracefully, he moved his body in movements of Taijiquan, which flowed easily like a river. Each scanned the landscape for a glimpse of the Archer. Their faces gnarled with panic, for he was nowhere to be found. Tears began to flow, and heartbeats became rapid. The younger archers wondered if he was now but a spirit riding the mountain winds.

Bolin said, "He is here in the winds. Listen, you will hear his voice. He is here in the clouds that wash the sky; look beyond. He is the grass beneath your feet; feel him. He is in your eyes for all that you see; he sees too."

Bolin continued, "You are not only an observer of this place or of the stars you see that fill the night skies. You are instead viewed as a participant by the universe, making you one of the smallest atoms or particles of dust. You are part of the sweeping motion of life as it is this moment. Grasp it, and hold it close for all we have is the now."

Suddenly, darkness filled the skies as ominous clouds blew onto the mountain, looking like billowing towers of dark-gray smoke. The winds stirred to a mighty force. Bewilderment flooded them as they gathered together, not understanding what was happening. A crack of lightning ripped through the sky, followed by the roar of thunder, which shook from the valley floor to the highest point of the mountain range. Again, lightning struck near the small red house, which sent whipping sounds cracking like the explosion of a bomb. Fear pushed its limit, bringing some to their knees while others covered their heads, not wanting to see the phenomenon before them.

Bolin looked toward them and said to all, "A story was told by those who taught the Archer many years ago. According to the tale, he possesses facets like those of a diamond. His teaching is gentle, and his knowledge is from a place beyond reality. The masters said that the crack of lightning that shattered the sky was the sound of the Archer releasing the string on his bow, sending his arrow to rip through the atmosphere. And the mighty thunder booming from the floor of the mountains is his arrow piercing the target. Listen; he is here." The Archer's students stood mesmerized by Bolin's tale.

The skies calmed, and a hint of sun began to show her face. Moments later, from behind them, the swishing of the arrows came. Turning, the Archer stood before them. Their eyes captured the moment as each wondered if their own minds had manifested his return. The many years had not changed him. The only sign of passing time was the graying of his once blond hair to silver. His eyes were youthful and his spirit alive. He was dressed in the robes of a warrior; those Bolin had given him upon his return to the mountain. His bow was in one hand, and his sword was held tight to his hip. One golden arrow showed itself from behind his back, tucked inside the sashes tied to his waist.

There was great joy among them as they hugged their teacher and stared not believing their eyes. They had feared he was dead. The Archer looked at each of them, seeing the passing of time written on their faces. Some had graying hair while others had laugh lines around their eyes. He listened as they told tales of their adventures through life and of the passing of too many years. They were wonderful stories, and he was pleased, knowing each had implemented all the teachings he shared, both those of the bow and those that came from his heart.

"My life is better because of you. I learned to listen to myself and to others, accepting all as it is. In this, I have grown so much under your silent care," said Giovanna.

The Archer turned to the couple who stood with a young boy. The woman looked into his eyes, and he realized that Meifeng looked very much like her mother, Lihua. From behind, a hand rested on his shoulder and a voice said, "It is me, Archer. Zu-Ling, husband of the one standing before you. Meet our son, Armin, whom we have named in your honor."

Tears came to the Archer's eyes as he learned of this news. The remainder of his students shared with him the mysteries of their lives and the deep-rooted sense of self, which they had come to know through his earlier teachings.

The day was nearing its end, and the sun began its slow sinking behind westerly mountain peaks. Silently, the women and men stood back-to-back, forming a circle looking outward to the world. Zu-Ling walked around to each one, bowed, and presented a bow to his fellow archers. As they accepted the bow offering, deep guttural sounds of thunder roared in the lower valley as if the heavens anticipated this sacred moment. Placing their golden arrows upon their bowstrings, they aligned their bodies and connected to their breathing cycle, as the Archer had taught so many years earlier. One by one, they raised their bows to the heavens, taking aim upon an invisible target. A crack of lightning whipped through the sky as the archers released their arrows into space, letting their spirits soar. It was their hope that others might find their arrows and the messages left behind. In this, they too would learn the truth of life and a better way of understanding humanity.

After a brief moment of silence, they turned to face their teacher, hoping their act would bring him joy. He was gone. Eyes searched the surrounding area for him as Salina and Sishiba ran to the small red house. Coach Armin was not there.

From nowhere, high-pitched shrills echoed throughout the mountains, sending waves of chills through their bodies. Stretching their faces toward the heavens, Fredric and the others saw not one but two magnificent Silverhawk's circling overhead. "Could it be?" Fredric softly wondered aloud. Just then, one of the hawks swooped down as he circled closely around them, stirring a breeze powerful enough to move the hair on their heads. Then, a brilliant light illuminated, sending hues of gold upon them as the Great Spirit ascended the skies, rejoining the ancient sage. Together, they glided on raising air currents off into a new celestial dimension. Their mighty cries lingered, echoing between the mountains and the lower valleys until they were no more. Once again, a wash of chills consumed each of the archers. Sudden gasps from Andrew took their attention out of their spellbinding trance. The Archer's bow had fallen to the earth. Next to it, one golden arrow lay on the face of Mother Earth, glistening in the late afternoon sun. Andrew ran to pick up what had been left behind by their beloved teacher. Knowing the Archer had left this arrow especially for him, he raised his voice so the others could hear and read aloud . . .

*"You have found your way."*

Never go where
The path may lead.
Go instead where
There is no path
And leave behind a trail.

—Ralph Waldo Emerson

Do not ask me
Where I am going
As I travel in this
Limitless world,
Where every step I take
is my home.

~~~~~Dogen~~~~~

January 19th 2014

My Dear Linda

Thank you for all
the years of support & for
our wonderful friendship

I Love You

Sissy

Carol Cottone Choomack ♡

CPSIA information can be obtained at www.ICGtesting.com
Printed in the USA
LVOW12s0422031213

363602LV00004B/16/P